DISGUSTING & DREADFUL SCIENCE

Gut-Wrenching Gravity

and other fatal forces

by Anna Claybourne

 Crabtree Publishing Company

www.crabtreebooks.com

Crabtree Publishing Company
www.crabtreebooks.com
1-800-387-7650

Published in Canada
Crabtree Publishing
616 Welland Avenue
St. Catharines, ON
L2M 5V6

Published in the USA
Crabtree Publishing
PMB 59051
350 Fifth Ave, 59th Floor
New York, NY 10118

Printed in Hong Kong/092012/BK20120629

Author: Anna Claybourne
Editorial director: Kathy Middleton
Editors: Nicola Edwards, Adrianna Morganelli
Proofreader: Crystal Sikkens
Designer: Elaine Wilkinson
Picture Researcher: Clive Gifford
**Production coordinator and
   Prepress technician:** Ken Wright
Print coordinator: Katherine Berti

Published by Crabtree Publishing in 2013

First published in 2013 by Franklin Watts
Copyright © Franklin Watts 2013

Picture acknowledgements:
Corbis images: 17b (Justin Paget). **fotolia:** 4b (Eduard Härkönen), 16t
(Dan Moller), 18b (Nickolae), 19t and cover (sarah5), 26b (pegbes),
26t (Henrik Larsson), 27tl (Dmitry Ersler), 27tr (Thomas Beitz). **Getty
images:** 25b (AFP/Fabrice Coffrini), 24t (The Image Bank/Windsor &
Wiehahn). iStockphoto.com: title page (Dean Murray), eyeball cartoon
(Elaine Barker), 4r (jesse christoffersen), 5b (pidjoe), 7bl (CactuSoup),
8l (Eric Isselée), 8r (hudiemm), 9t (Ugurhan Betin), 9br (TriggerPhoto),
10b (Sébastien Decoret), 10t and cover (Aleksander Trankov), 11b (Linda
Bucklin), 13b and cover (Sven Hermann), 20t (Christian Martínez Kempin),
22t (Tommounsey), **NASA:** 14b, 19bl, 27bl, 28t, 28b, 29b. **Science Photo
Library:** 15r (Victor Habbick Visions), 29t (Mark Williamson). **Shutterstock.
com:** angry monster cartoon (Yayayoyo), 5tr and cover (Philippe Ingels),
5tl (Africa Studio), 6–7 (HomeArt), 7tr (Sergej Khakimullin), 9 mouse (Don
Purcell), 11t (Kapu), 12b and cover (jabiru), 14t (CoraMax), 15b (Yingko),
18t (Nickolay Vinokurov), 21c (Joe Belanger), 21t (grafoto), 21b (Stuart
Elflett), 23c (xpixel), 23b (Hung Chung Chih), 24b (creativedoxfoto).
Wikimedia: 11 – Louis XVI, 13r, 25t.

All other illustrations by Graham Rich

Every attempt has been made to clear copyright. Should there be any
inadvertent omission, please apply to the publisher for rectification.

**Library and Archives Canada
Cataloguing in Publication**

Claybourne, Anna
Claybourne, Anna
     Gut-wrenching gravity and other fatal forces / Anna Claybourne.

(Disgusting and dreadful science)
Includes index.
Issued also in electronic format.
ISBN 978-0-7787-0957-2 (pbk.).--ISBN 978-0-7787-0950-3 (bound)

     1. Gravity--Juvenile literature. I. Title. II. Series: Disgusting and
dreadful science

QC178.C53 2013   j531'.14   C2012-907291-5

**Library of Congress
Cataloging-in-Publication Data**

CIP available at Library of Congress

Contents

Feel the force!

Oops! **CRUNCH!** Ouch! If you trip over your shoelaces and go flying, you soon fall flat on your face. You are dragged violently toward the ground by a fearsome force called gravity. Gravity acts like a **PULLING** force. So when you fall over, you really are being pulled to the ground.

We'll force you!

Gravity is just one of the forces that pull, push, squeeze, and shove us around, all day long. We're so used to these forces, we often don't notice them – but they affect everything we do. Here are a few you might recognize...

PUSH – when you kick a ball, you push it with your foot

PULL – when you pull your socks up to get them onto your feet

SQUEEZE – when you SQUELCH a handful of slime between your fingers

STRE-E-ETCH – when you pull an elastic band, then fling it across the room

SCRAPE – when your chair scrapes on the floor with an ear-splitting screech!

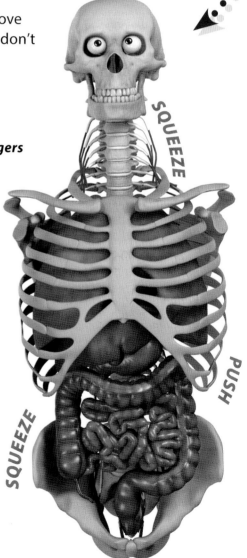

Pushes and pulls make your body work, too. Muscles PULL to make your bones move. When you eat, tubes SQUEEZE tight to PUSH the food along — and to PUSH out your poo!

SQUEEZE

PUSH

SQUEEZE

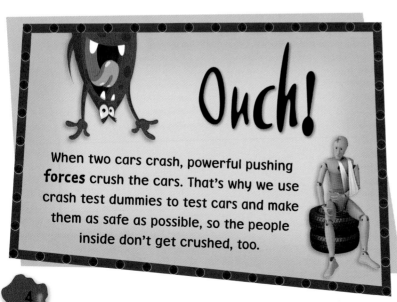

Ouch!

When two cars crash, powerful pushing **forces** crush the cars. That's why we use crash test dummies to test cars and make them as safe as possible, so the people inside don't get crushed, too.

Balanced forces

If an object isn't moving, it's because the forces acting on it are balanced. If a cake sits on a plate, gravity is pulling it down, but the plate is in the way and stops the cake from falling. The plate is actually pushing it up. The two forces balance each other and the cake stays still.

See for Yourself

Diving board

Hold a wooden or plastic ruler over the edge of a table, and stand a toy figure on the end. Gently pull down the tip of the ruler, then let it go.

You PULL down on the ruler. The ruler springs back and PUSHES the figure up. After a daring leap, gravity PULLS the figure to the ground.

Wheee!

Unbalanced forces

Who do you think will win this arm wrestle?

If the pushing forces are unbalanced, the stronger force will push the weaker one.

The mystery of gravity

Gravity is everywhere. It makes an egg splat on the floor when you drop it. It makes snot dribble out of your nose. It lets you pour juice into a glass, play ball games, and have a shower. Gravity can be a drag when you're carrying a heavy bag, but it can be fun, when you're sledding, skiing, or skydiving.

I'm floating away!

Imagine life without gravity! Nothing would stay where you put it. You couldn't walk down the street—you'd just float around. The air would be filled with random objects. Except there wouldn't be any air, either! Gravity holds air in place around our planet, allowing us to breathe. So, as you can see, it's pretty important.

 6

A universe of gravity

Everything on Earth is pulled toward the center of the planet by gravity, but it's not just Earth that has gravity. Every object—including the Moon, a pebble, a pea, and you yourself—has a pulling force that draws it toward other objects. The more massive an object is, the more powerful its gravity. Small objects have such weak gravity we don't notice it, but Earth's gravity is so strong it pulls on us and everything else nearby.

On Earth, there's actually no such thing as "down."

How does it do it?

How can one object pull on another across empty space? Where exactly does the pulling power of gravity come from? The truth is... wait for it... we don't actually know! Gravity is a massive mystery. The world's greatest minds are still trying to figure out why it's there and how it works.

Splatttt!

Yuck!

Scientists have found that when toast falls off a table, it really does usually land on the buttery side. That's because, as it tips off the table, it starts to spin. In the time it takes gravity to pull the toast to the floor, it only has time to spin 180 degrees, or half a full turn—so it's upside-down when it lands.

Splat!

Stand back! Cow dung (below) can make a mighty splat as it hits the ground! The further something falls, the bigger the mess when it lands. As an object falls toward Earth, it speeds up, or accelerates. The longer it falls for, the faster it falls. That's why you can jump off a low wall and land safely (most of the time!), but what if you fell off a high cliff?

Some birds use the splatting power of gravity to help them bombard their enemies with sticky, slimy droppings.

Faster... faster... faster

On Earth, falling objects speed up by 32 feet (9.8 metres) per second. That's quite a lot—equivalent to about 22 mph (35 km/h). With each second that passes, the object falls 22 mph (35 km/h) faster. As you can imagine, after just a few seconds, a falling object is zooming as fast as a speeding train.

Floaty and Fluffy

The speed of a falling object is affected by **air resistance**—that is, air getting in its way. Light, fluffy objects like feathers catch a lot of air, which slows them down, but a rock or a person falls much faster. If there was no air resistance, a feather and a rock would fall at the same speed.

Drop it!

Imagine you climbed up a 328-foot (100-meter) skyscraper, and dropped a rotten tomato off the top.

AFTER 1 SECOND
Your tomato is already moving faster than you could run! It's falling at

22 mph (35 km/h)

AFTER 2 SECONDS
It's just past

44 mph (79 km/h)

AFTER 3 SECONDS
It's plummeting down at almost

66 mph (106 km/h)

AFTER 4 SECONDS
Your tomato is travelling at a breakneck speed of

87 mph (140 km/h)

Then it hits the ground...

SPLAT!

See for Yourself

Water balloon splats

Fill several balloons with water (use the same amount of water for each one) and tie them closed. Then try dropping them from different heights off the ground—1.6 feet (0.5 meters), 3.3 feet (1 meter) and 4.9 feet (1.5 meters) (*you'll need to go outside for this!*). How far does a balloon have to fall to make it splat? Can you make a bigger splat by dropping it from higher up? To get your balloons even higher, throw them up in the air. Record your results on a chart, like this.

	Height	Diameter of splat
1st drop	1.6 feet (0.5 m)	No splat
2nd drop	3.3 feet (1 m)	?
3rd drop	4.9 feet (1.5 m)	?

Don't forget to clean up the pieces of balloon afterward. They can be dangerous to wildlife.

Deadly gravity

Living with gravity can be **DREADFULLY** dangerous. Whether it's you falling over, or something falling on top of you, gravity's pulling force can cause all kinds of deadly disasters.

Aarrrrgggghhhh!

Base jumpers and skydivers throw themselves out of airplanes or off cliffs and mountains for fun. Falls of more than 49 feet (15 meters) without a parachute are usually deadly for humans, but some people are lucky. During the Second World War (1939-45), British Royal Air Force gunner Nick Alkemade jumped from his burning plane. He fell about 18,045 feet (5,500 meters) and prepared to die. Instead, a pine tree broke his fall and he landed in soft snow. He was unhurt except for a sprained ankle.

A skydiver in free fall, enjoying the pull of Earth's gravity

Falling from space

Sometimes, pieces of rock flying through space come close enough to Earth to be pulled in by its gravity. They often burn up as they fall through the atmosphere and we see them as "shooting stars." Some, called **meteorites**, fall all the way to Earth. If they hit someone, it could be deadly. In 2009, a pea-sized meteorite hit 14-year-old Gerrit Blank as he walked to school in Germany. Luckily he wasn't badly hurt. If a really big space rock, or **asteroid** (left), hit us it could wipe out life on Earth!

Get out of the way!

Gravity often causes terrifying natural disasters. It pulls floodwater, avalanches, landslides, and extremely hot volcanic lava downhill. The further they flow, the faster they go, flattening anything in their path.

Snow might be fun, but an avalanche is terrifying and deadly when it's hurtling toward you at over 99 mph (59 km/h)!

Fatal fall

In the past, the **guillotine** was used to **behead** criminals —and sometimes kings and queens! The guillotine's sharp, heavy blade was pulled up into a high position using a rope. When it was let go, gravity pulled the blade down. **CHOP!**

SACRE BLEU!

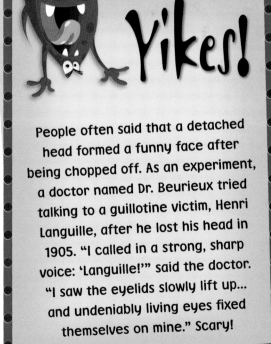

Yikes!

People often said that a detached head formed a funny face after being chopped off. As an experiment, a doctor named Dr. Beurieux tried talking to a guillotine victim, Henri Languille, after he lost his head in 1905. "I called in a strong, sharp voice: 'Languille!'" said the doctor. "I saw the eyelids slowly lift up... and undeniably living eyes fixed themselves on mine." Scary!

11

Gut-wrenching g-forces

You might have heard of fighter pilots and racecar drivers enduring massive "g-forces." Strong g-forces can make you feel dizzy, throw up, collapse unconscious, and even die! So, what are

See for Yourself

Feel super gravity

Stand on a bathroom scale. Make a small jump and land back on the scale. *(Be careful! Just do a small jump so you don't break it.)* Look at the scale as you land and you'll see it show an increased reading as you decelerate and your g-force goes up. The same thing sometimes happens when you're in an elevator and it lands on the ground floor.

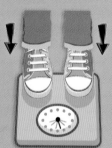

Extra gravity

The "g" in **g-force** stands for gravity and 1g means the force of gravity you feel on Earth. A force of 2g means twice the force of Earth's gravity, and so on. When you accelerate (speed up) or **decelerate** (slow down), you feel a pushing force. In an airplane, you feel "pushed" back into your seat at take off. On a bus, you are pushed forward if it stops suddenly. These are g-forces. When we experience them, we feel a force greater than gravity.

Wheeee!

You experience g-forces when you race up and down on a rollercoaster, or when you're in a car that turns a corner quickly, pushing you sideways. If you fall, then hit the ground, your body experiences multiple gs as you suddenly decelerate.

AAGGGHHH!

Ouch!

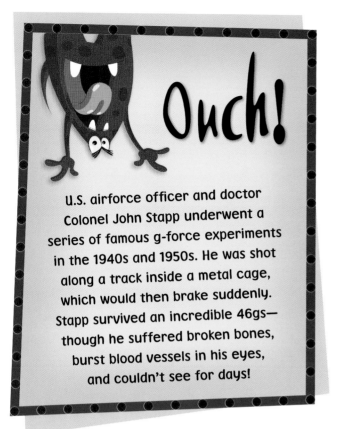

U.S. airforce officer and doctor Colonel John Stapp underwent a series of famous g-force experiments in the 1940s and 1950s. He was shot along a track inside a metal cage, which would then brake suddenly. Stapp survived an incredible 46gs—though he suffered broken bones, burst blood vessels in his eyes, and couldn't see for days!

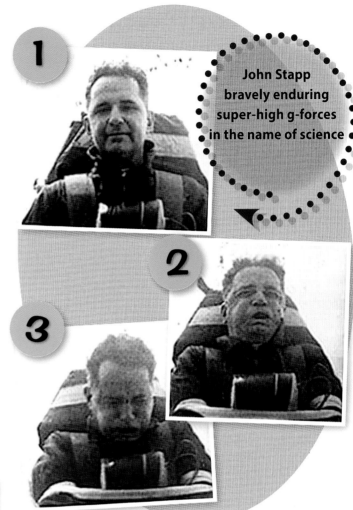

1

2

3

John Stapp bravely enduring super-high g-forces in the name of science

SUPER-G STATS

Space shuttle during a launch	**3g**
Rollercoaster	**3–5g**
Formula-1 racing car turning	**up to 6g**
Fighter jet turning	**up to 12g**
Car crash at 31 mph (50 km/h)	**25g**

High g-forces are all in a day's work for fighter pilots and racecar drivers.

G-force machine!

Pilots of fast planes undergo high g-forces as they accelerate, twist, and turn. To help them get used to it, they are whirled around in a human centrifuge machine, which spins faster than any carnival ride to create huge g-forces. As the gs increase, the pilot first suffers "grey-out" (loss of color vision), then **tunnel vision**, complete blindness, and finally "GLOC"– g-force induced loss of consciousness. **Urgh!**

13

Falling forever

Imagine falling... and falling... and falling... but never hitting the ground! Well, that's what planet Earth is doing right now and it's taking you with it. We are orbiting **around the Sun, and orbiting is basically falling. It happens because of gravity.**

Moon's forward motion

Pull of Earth's gravity

Resulting path (orbit)

How does it work?

Think of our Moon orbiting around us. The Moon moves at a certain speed, but it is also close enough to the planet to be pulled by its gravity. The Moon is constantly trying to keep going in a straight line, but the planet's gravity pulls on it, making it fall toward Earth. These two forces balance each other out, and the Moon ends up moving around and around the planet—always falling, but never landing.

The same forces are also at work on the International Space Station and astronauts, such as this one, on spacewalks.

Gravity glue

Gravity holds the whole **solar system** together. The huge Sun is in the middle, and its mighty gravity holds the planets in orbit. The planets each have their own moon or moons orbiting around them.

See for Yourself

Make a moon

You can see how a moon's orbit works by whirling a ball on a string. Place a tennis ball inside a long sock or nylon pantyhose, and push it to the end. Holding the other end of the sock, spin the ball around (first making sure no one is in the way). The speed of the ball makes it pull away from you. But the sock acts like gravity, holding the ball in place. It ends up moving around in a circle.

The big squeeze

One of Jupiter's moons, Io (right), is like a big pimple. Jupiter's super-strong gravity squeezes it so much it squirts out goop from inside through its many volcanoes.

Ouch!

Medieval weapons like the chain mace used orbiting forces, too. The chain held the mace ball, while it whirled around at great speed, before making contact with someone's head!

15

Stretched into spaghetti

Earth's gravity is strong. Jupiter's gravity is stronger. The Sun's gravity is stronger still. But to experience the most powerful gravity of all, you'd have to brave something much stranger – the mysterious depths of a black hole.

What's a black hole?

Black holes (above) are strange space objects where gravity is taken to the extreme. They suck in space dust, gas, comets, pieces of stars, and even light. Their gravity is so strong that nothing that gets sucked in can ever escape. Instead, it all gets squashed together more and more tightly, until it's smaller than a pinprick – but heavier than a star. Mind boggling!

Yikes!

Black holes sound scary. What if Earth gets sucked into one? Don't panic! The nearest black holes are many millions of meters away and, although their gravity is very strong, they only pull in objects that get close enough.

16

Where do black holes come from?

Massive star

Red supergiant

Supernova

Black hole

A black hole forms when a very big star runs out of fuel. At the end of its life it expands to form a red supergiant. Then it explodes, forming a supernova as its gravity forces it to collapse in on itself. It pulls itself into a clump of **matter** that is very dense—meaning it's very heavy for its size. Its strong gravity sucks in more and more matter, until it becomes a black hole. Black holes get their name because they even suck in light, so they appear black.

Getting sucked in

Slurp! Slurp!

If you fell into a black hole feet first, the super-strong gravity would pull harder on your feet than on your head, as your feet would be nearest to it. This would make your body stretch as you got sucked in – an effect scientists call "**spaghettification**." Luckily, though, no one has actually fallen into a black hole... yet!

See for Yourself

The drains of space

Run some water into a plugged sink, then take the plug out. As the water swirls down the drain, sprinkle some glitter and a few tiny pieces of tissue paper around it. You'll see them swirl around the hole and move faster and faster as they get sucked in. A black hole works in a similar way. Scientists can't see them, but they can detect them from the way nearby objects move around the black hole.

Gravity geeks

We may not yet understand gravity completely, but we know a lot more than we used to. That's thanks to the brilliant brains of these gravity-studying geniuses.

Mind your head!

People used to think heavy objects fell faster than light objects. Some light objects, like feathers, do fall slowly, but this is because of air resistance—air getting trapped and holding them up. The great scientist Galileo saw that if it wasn't for air resistance gravity should pull all objects at the same rate. In 1589, according to legend, he tried dropping two weights, one ten times heavier than the other, off the Leaning Tower of Pisa (right). He proved his point! As they were both solid and heavy, air resistance had little effect, and they both landed at the same time.

10 TON

1 TON

BOING!

Over to Isaac

Galileo died in 1642, and in that same year Isaac Newton was born. Newton was probably the most brilliant scientist ever. He worked out that gravity made orbits work, and that everything had gravity, not just Earth. Some people say he "discovered" gravity when an apple fell on his head—but of course everyone already knew that objects fell downward. They just didn't understand what was going on in the same way Newton did.

18

Isaac Newton (1642–1727)

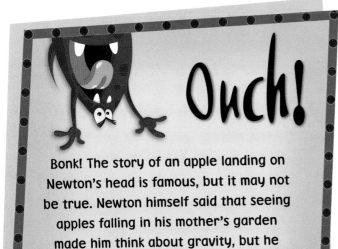

Ouch!

Bonk! The story of an apple landing on Newton's head is famous, but it may not be true. Newton himself said that seeing apples falling in his mother's garden made him think about gravity, but he didn't say they fell on his head. He simply questioned why they didn't fall sideways or upward, but always toward Earth's center.

Einstein

The great physicist Albert Einstein said that gravity happens because matter bends space and time, so that smaller objects fall "in" toward it. It's hard to understand, but this experiment might help...

Moon test

When the first astronauts walked on the Moon (above), they tested Galileo's theory. They dropped a metal weight and a feather to test whether they fell at the same speed when there was no air resistance at all. They both landed at the same time, just as Galileo predicted they would.

See for Yourself

Bending space

Try testing Einstein's idea by stretching out a piece of stretchy fabric over the top of a big bowl. Secure it tightly with a large elastic band or tape. Put a big marble in the center of the fabric. What happens? Try rolling marbles of different sizes and weights across the fabric. Can you explain what is happening and why?

The big marble is like a planet bending space (the stretchy fabric). The smaller marbles (a moon, an asteroid, or a spacecraft) "fall in'" when they get close enough to the planet's gravity.

Note: This experiment uses a flat surface, but in reality the "bending" would work in all directions.

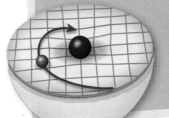

Frightening friction

Friction is a dragging force that happens when things rub against each other. It can cause some painful injuries, like when you scrape your knee, get a massive blister from your shoe, or burn your hands sliding down a rope—OUCH! But if it weren't for friction, every day would be like walking on ice!

But what is friction?

Friction happens when two surfaces are in contact and trying to move past each other. They catch and rub, and slow each other down. This can damage them, and it also uses up energy. Rough or squishy surfaces, like sandpaper and rubber, have more friction. Smooth, shiny surfaces, like glass, have less.

Yuck!

When things are covered with water, oil, or slime, there's less friction because the liquid gets between the two surfaces. For example, snails make slippery slime to help them slither along the ground. Deep-sea hagfish release a lot of slime to make it harder for predators to grab and catch them.

A snail's slime helps it to overcome friction, but wheels are even better!

Wheels make it easier to move around because they don't rub—they roll instead, making friction less of a problem.

Friction and heat

When friction happens, some of the movement energy gets turned into heat, and the surfaces warm up. That's why your hands warm up when you rub them together on a cold day. Heat from friction is used to strike matches, and also lets you start a fire by rubbing sticks together.

Racecars use smooth tires in dry weather, and tires with rough treads in the rain. The rough treads give them extra friction.

 ## See for Yourself

Feel the heat

1. Take two identical coins and put them both on a pad of paper. Hold one still, and rub the other one quickly to and fro for 30 seconds. Which one ends up warmer?

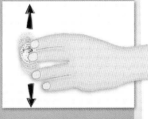

Without friction

2. Fill a large, smooth plastic bottle with water, dry it, and see if you can hold it up in one hand. Now spread a thin layer of vegetable oil all over it. Is it still as easy to hold?

Magnet mayhem

A magnet can defy gravity. It can pull objects up toward it, or push another magnet into the air. So the force of magnetism can actually make things seem to "float" instead of fall. How does it do that?

What is a magnet?

A magnet is an object, usually a metal bar, disk, or U-shape, that has a magnetic field—an area of force around it. It can **attract**, or pull, some things toward it—especially anything made of iron, steel, or nickel. Two magnets can attract each other, or **repel** (push away from) each other. Just like gravity, these forces can reach across empty space.

Magnets sometimes occur naturally. They can also be made from a magnetic material such as iron. In a magnet, the **atoms**—the tiny parts that all things are made of—are arranged in a regular pattern that gives the magnet its force. A flow of electricity can also create a magnetic force.

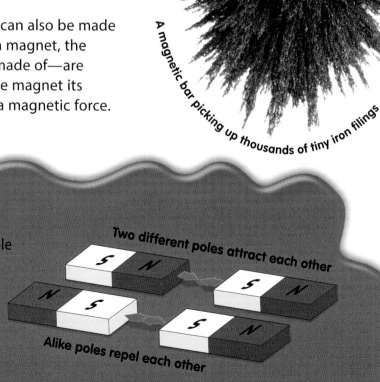

A magnetic bar picking up thousands of tiny iron filings

Magnets

One end of a magnet is called the north pole and the other is called the south pole. When two magnets are put together, north and south ends will pull together and connect. If you try to put two south poles or two north poles together, they push away. They will not connect.

Two different poles attract each other

Alike poles repel each other

North pole? South pole? Do those terms sound familiar? That's because Earth is a giant magnet too, and has its own North Pole and South Pole.

North magnetic pole

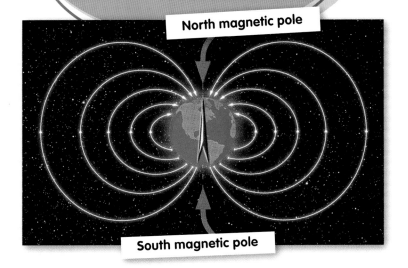

South magnetic pole

Ouch!

Magnets can be seriously scary. Very strong magnets called neodymium magnets can pull together so violently that they can crush your fingers, like a pair of pliers, when they attract (come together). Strong magnets can also make metal objects fly through the air toward them. They can even be deadly if they are swallowed, as they cling together and can damage your insides.

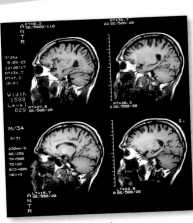

MRI

An MRI scanner uses magnetism to make chemicals in your body change position, then turns their movements into an image. It's often used to scan people's brains.

An MRI brain scan

Beware the power!

A super-speedy "**maglev**" train (left) uses magnets to help it move. Strong magnetic forces make the train hover above a magnetic rail, so friction never slows it down. Other magnets, powered by electricity, make the train move. Similar technology could be used in the future to move other things around, too. In the *X-Men* comics and films, the villain Magneto uses his magnetic powers as a weapon. He controls huge metal objects like ships—though this doesn't happen in real life (yet!)

23

Floating, flying, and gravity-defying

Humans have always longed to leave the ground, like birds and insects do. It took us a long time, but we eventually invented several ways to defy gravity and fly.

Personal jet-packs – the future or just a dream?

See for Yourself

Flying hands

Planes fly because the wings are slightly tilted. As they zoom forward, air hits the underside of the wing and is pushed down. This pushes the plane up.

To demonstrate this, use a hairdryer on a cool setting to blow air at your hand.

First, hold your hand out flat.

Now try tilting your hand like this. Can you feel it being pushed up by the airflow? This is how aircraft wings get pushed up, too.

COOL AIR!

Hot air!

The first passenger-carrying flying machine, a huge hot-air balloon, took to the air in 1783. Hot-air balloons work by floating. Cold air is heavier than hot air, so cold air sinks down (pulled by gravity), and pushes hot air up. If the balloon is big enough, and the air inside is hot enough, it can carry people into the sky.

Balloons and airships are sometimes filled with lighter-than-air gases, such as helium. Like hot air, these gases make the balloon float upward, while the heavier air sinks down.

Wonderful wings

Long ago, people tried to fly by copying birds and building big, flapping wings—but they were too heavy and it didn't work. When inventors tried using fixed, spread-out wings, like a gliding eagle, airplanes were born. The first planes were gliders with no engines. They were launched off hills. The first powered plane flew in 1903.

Otto Lilienthal was known as the Glider King for his fantastic flying machines.

Ouch!

In 1507, an inventor named John Damian made himself a pair of wings from eagle and chicken feathers. He tried to fly from the top of a tower, but fell straight into a sloppy, stinky pile of manure!

Is it a bird? Is it a plane?

This superhuman-looking high-speed flyer is actually pilot and inventor Yves Rossy, wearing his custom-built, jet-engine-powered wing suit. His invention lets one person fly like a bird, but only he has flown in it so far. It works like a miniature plane, with fixed wings that allow it to fly and glide. In 2008, Rossy used his flying suit to cross the English Channel, a journey of 22 miles (35 km).

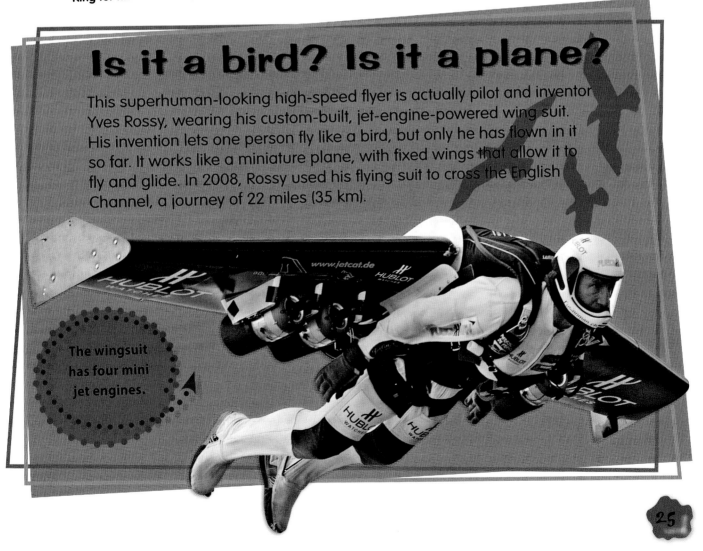

The wingsuit has four mini jet engines.

25

Crawling on the ceiling

If gravity affects everything on Earth, how do spiders, flies, and lizards crawl across the ceiling? Have you ever wondered that? After all, we can't walk on walls and ceilings. So what have creepy crawlies got that we haven't?

Even if a wall looks smooth, it will probably have tiny bumps and cracks in it. Spiders have tiny claws on their feet that they use to cling onto the wall. Since a spider is very light and has eight legs to use, it can usually get a good grip. But spiders walk up windows, too. **How do they do that?**

A spider can have over 70,000 tiny hairs on each foot.

Gripping hairs!

Through a microscope you'd see that spiders' feet are covered in tiny hairs. Each of these hairs has hundreds of tinier hairs, called setae. But how do hairs help?

When you touch a surface with your fingertip, you don't actually touch much of it at all. Your finger and the surface have different textures, and close up, only some parts actually touch. When a spider touches a surface with its hairy feet, each tiny hair makes contact.

AAGGGHH!

26

Sticking power

Weak electrical forces, called **Van der Waals forces**, attract surfaces together. They are so weak we rarely feel them, but the hairs on a spider's feet make such close contact with a surface, the Van der Waals forces are strong enough to make it stick. Gecko's feet are hairy too, and work in the same way.

GECKO toes!

Besides being covered in tiny setae, a gecko's toes are wide and rounded, to give them a bigger gripping area.

Gecko's toe hairs (setae) —

Gecko's toe

Surface

Spiders in space!

Spiders have been sent into space aboard rockets to see if they could still spin their webs in zero gravity (above). They could!

Yuck!

If you've ever walked into a cobweb, you'll know it's stretchy, sticky, and icky! Spiders use their silk to spin webs and catch prey, but also to hang down from ceilings. To fix the silk to a ceiling, a spider wraps several threads into a sticky bundle called an attachment disk, and presses it into place. Then it dangles from the other end. Watch out!

All aboard the vomit comet!

Flying is amazing when you think about it – being thousands of miles in the air in a small metal tube with wings, eating and drinking and watching TV. But imagine what it would be like to experience ZERO gravity* and float around almost weightless.

*Ahem!

There's actually no such thing as true zero gravity. Gravity gets weaker and weaker with distance, but it never disappears completely. All objects have their own gravity, so we are never free of it. The correct term for very low gravity is "**microgravity**."

Yuck!

On the International Space Station, astronauts stay for so long, they can't take all their drinking water with them. Instead, they have a system that cleans and recycles their urine so they can drink it again!

Into space

Astronauts in orbit experience microgravity on their missions (top). Floating around and doing somersaults is fun, but space can also be seriously messy. Any spilt food or drink ends up flying around all over the place (above).

Astronaut poo!

So how do astronauts go to the toilet? Imagine everything from your toilet at home floating around all over the room! Space toilets solve this problem using a suction system. As you sit on the toilet, air is sucked out of it, and everything else gets sucked away, too. The poo is dried out, then stored in a sealed container to be taken back to Earth.

• This is the hole for solid "waste" (that's poo).

• This is the urine funnel. It's flexible so both men and women can use it. This iquid waste is treated and recycled.

• Air suction does the job that gravity does on Earth. It pulls the waste into the toilet.

• A fan separates the waste from the air using centrifugal force.

• The air is treated to remove odors and bacteria before it is released back into the room.

• The solid waste goes into plastic bags inside the toilet, which are squashed flat.

The vomit comet

The vomit comet is the nickname for a plane that can create a gravity-free experience for trainee astronauts. It works by climbing up high, then plummeting downward at the same speed as free fall. The people inside are falling, but the plane is falling with them—so, for a few minutes, it is just like being weightless inside a spacecraft.

Why "vomit comet"? Because the experience of weightlessness often makes people horribly sick. Everyone is given a special vomit bag, just in case!

WWHHHEEEEEE!

BLEUURRGGH!

Glossary

accelerate To speed up

air resistance Air that is in the way of a moving object slowing it down

asteroid A rocky space object that orbits the Sun

atoms Tiny units that all things are made of

attract To pull on something

base jumpers People who jump off objects, such as mountains and buildings, wearing wingsuits and parachutes

behead To cut someone's head off

black hole A space object with very strong gravity that sucks nearby material into it

decelerate To slow down

force A push or pull acting on an object

g-force The force of gravity or acceleration on an object

guillotine A machine for beheading people using a falling blade

maglev (short for magnetic levitation) A type of train that uses magnetic force to move and to hover above the track

matter The stuff that makes up objects and substances

meteorite A lump of rock or metal from space that falls and lands on Earth's surface

microgravity Very low gravity

orbit To circle around an object, held in place by its gravity

physicist A scientist who studies physics

repel To push something away

solar system The Sun and all the planets and other space objects that orbit around it

spaghettification A stretching effect that acts on objects that are sucked into a black hole

tunnel vision Being able to see only a small area right in front of you

Van der Waals force A weak pulling force between objects

Websites and Places to visit

NASA Kids' Club
www.nasa.gov/audience/forkids/kidsclub/
flash/index.html
A lot of fun activities and facts about space
exploration, rockets, and astronauts

Microgravity water balloons
spaceflightsystems.grc.nasa.gov/
WaterBalloon
A series of cool videos showing how water
behaves in microgravity

Science Kids – Forces in Action
www.sciencekids.co.nz/gamesactivities/
forcesinaction.html
An interactive truck game that lets
you experiment with friction and
other forces

Zoom Science – Forces & Energy
pbskids.org/zoom/activities/sci
The Forces & Energy section has lots of
fun and fascinating force-related
experiments to try

thinktank
Birmingham Science Museum
and Planetarium
Millennium Point, Curzon Street,
Birmingham B4 7XG
www.thinktank.ac

At-Bristol
Anchor Road, Harbourside,
Bristol BS1 5DB
www.at-bristol.org.uk

**Smithsonian National Air and
Space Museum**
National Mall Building:
Independence Avenue at 6th Street,
SW Washington, DC 20560, U.S.A.
www.nasm.si.edu

Canada Science and Technology Museum
1867 St. Laurent Blvd.
Ottawa, Ontario K1G 5A3
Canada
www.sciencetechnomuses.ca/english/
index.cfm

Center of Science and Industry
333 W. Broad Street
Columbus, OH 43215 U.S.A.
www.cosi.org

Exploratorium
3601 Lyon Street
San Francisco, CA 94123 U.S.A.
www.exploratorium.edu/

Liberty Science Center
Liberty State Park
222 Jersey City Boulevard
Jersey City, NJ 07305 U.S.A.
www.lsc.org

Steven F. Udvar-Hazy Center
14390 Air and Space Museum
Parkway, Chantilly, VA 20151, U.S.A.

Index

From the Scottish Highlands to the courts of Versailles to the eastern shores of North America, the TV show *Outlander* brings to life in gorgeous detail the epic love story of Jamie Fraser and Claire Beauchamp Randall. Now knitters of all skill levels can knit 20 projects of apparel, accessories, and home décor that take inspiration from memorable episodes. Knit the capelet cowl that Mrs. Fitz gives to Claire at Castle Leoch, warm your feet with Clan MacKenzie Boot Socks, swaddle your bairn with the Mo Chridhe Baby Blanket, and dress your Jamie in a warm waistcoat. Highlighting everything from chunky knits to Celtic cables, each project includes a clearly written pattern, gorgeous photography, and a scene from the show's set. A love letter to the fans, *Outlander Knitting* will transport you back in time to the Scottish Highlands.

OUTLANDER
Knitting

THE
OFFICIAL BOOK
OF
20 Knits
INSPIRED BY THE HIT SERIES

EDITED BY KATE ATHERLEY
PHOTOGRAPHS BY GALE ZUCKER

CLARKSON POTTER/PUBLISHERS
NEW YORK

Published in the United States by Clarkson Potter/Publishers, an imprint of Random
House, a division of Penguin Random House LLC, New York.
clarksonpotter.com

CLARKSON POTTER is a trademark and POTTER
with colophon is a registered trademark of
Penguin Random House LLC.

Library of Congress Cataloging-in-Publication Data
Names: Atherley, Kate, editor. | Zucker, Gale, illustrator.
Title: Outlander knitting : the official book of 20 knits inspired by the hit series / edited
    by Kate Atherley ; photographs by Gale Zucker.
Description: New York : Clarkson Potter/Publishers, 2020. | Includes index. |
Identifiers: LCCN 2019053048 (print) | LCCN 2019053049 (ebook) | ISBN
    9780593138205 (hardcover) | ISBN 9780593138212 (ebook) | Subjects: LCSH:
    Knitting—Patterns. | Outlander (Television program)—Miscellanea. Classification:
    LCC TT825 .O956 2020 (print) | LCC TT825 (ebook) | DDC 746.43/2041—dc23
LC record available at https://lccn.loc.gov/2019053048
LC ebook record available at https://lccn.loc.gov/2019053049

ISBN 978-0-593-13820-5
Ebook ISBN 978-0-593-13821-2

Printed in China

Edited by Kate Atherley
Book and cover design by Francesca Truman
Book and cover photographs by Gale Zucker

10 9 8 7 6 5 4 3 2 1

First Edition

To the Fans

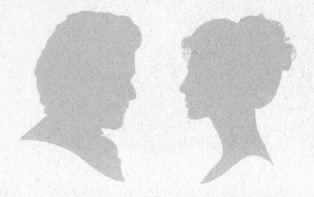

Contents

Introduction

※※※※※※※※

There are so many gorgeous things to enjoy in the *Outlander* TV series—including beautiful scenery, beautiful people, and a truly remarkable amount of beautiful knitwear. The crafters who have been watching the series have responded with such enthusiasm for the knits (and a few sneaky crocheted pieces) that many have created their own interpretations of the pieces they've seen on-screen. Well, this book is our love letter to the fans. We're right there with you, knitting in front of the TV, wishing we were in the Highlands instead.

The projects in this book were created by expert knitting designers and are a mix of homages to the costumes worn in the show and items inspired by characters or scenes. After all, even if we don't see one on-screen, we know that expert tea-leaf reader Mrs. Graham would need a cozy for her teapot.

There's also something here for every skill level and knitting interest. If you're a beginner knitter—or you're just looking for a relaxing knit to work on while catching up on missed episodes—you'll easily be able to tackle the Sassenach Capelet Cowl or the simplified version of the Rent Shawl; and if you're up for a wee bit of adventure, try Mrs. Fitz's Armwarmers. If you'd like to dip your toe into stranded colorwork, the Lovat Mitts and Cowl are the perfect projects. A more experienced stranded colorwork knitter will relish the Targe Tam. If you enjoy lacework, both the River Run Shawl and the Lace Fichu are satisfying projects, engaging but not too challenging. There are two sock designs that we didn't see on-screen, but we know very well indeed that you'd need warm socks while roaming the Highlands or tending your homestead in the New World. If you're looking for an heirloom-quality project using traditional techniques, consider the stranded colorwork and steeked The Man I Left Behind Vest.

Each pattern lists Skills Required so you'll know what techniques are needed that go above and beyond the basics of casting on, binding off, increasing and decreasing; this list will give you a sense of the complexity of each pattern. The Glossary and Techniques section at the back of the book is there to help you out with terms and techniques you might not know. If there's a special term for a particular pattern, we've listed that in the pattern instructions. All swatches should be blocked for determining gauge.

We hope you enjoy making (and wearing) these projects and that they transport you through the stones.

the Fandom

The knitting fever all started as a practical response to the weather in Scotland. The *Outlander* production crew—especially those hailing from California—quickly discovered how cold life can be in the Highlands, especially in drafty old stone houses. In preparing for the Castle Leoch scenes, the costume designers made a fateful snap decision, grabbing a piece of wool and wrapping it around Caitriona Balfe's neck. While all those extra skirts were keeping her legs warm, the necklines on eighteenth-century dresses were often too low for wintry weather. And it wasn't just neck wraps; fingerless mittens appear frequently in the first season.

The actors appreciated the warmth, and the fans appreciated seeing the nod to historical garb. Soon enough, knitters were creating their own versions of Claire's gorgeous cowl and Mrs. Fitz's practical mittens. Some of the knitwear was easily dissected, appearing front and center on-screen. Other pieces required a bit more detective work: many a knitter and fan spent time squinting at screenshots to work out the fine details of Frank's classic 1940s Fair Isle vest.

The costume team was initially surprised at the response, but quickly came to love the knitterly attention, seeing it as a sign of the fans' devotion to the show.

In later seasons, we can see hints that the team knows we're watching: at River Run, Aunt Jocasta and Phaedre are spotted knitting and there's a reappearance of a few favorite items, like the cowl Brianna wears in Wilmington, no doubt an homage to her mother in season 1.

Accessories

GATHERING
Cape

Designed by Anni Howard

In season 1, during the gathering of the MacKenzie clan, a hunting party ventures into the woods to hunt a wild boar with Claire in tow in case of any injuries—she wears this cape to protect her shoulders from the cold. Worked in a super-bulky warm wool roving yarn on large needles, this cape is easy and very quick to knit up, perfect for an impulsive exploration into the depths of the forest, or as a last-minute gift idea to share your love of *Outlander* with others.

SKILLS REQUIRED

Basic crochet stitches

MATERIALS

Trendsetter Yarns Me (100% superwash wool; 75yds/69m per 3.5oz/100g skein); 3 (3, 4) skeins
Sample uses color 340/Rustic Romance.

Substitution Notes: The chosen yarn is a slubby, super-bulky, 100% merino roving yarn with colors printed on top. Look for something with similar texture and coloring.

NEEDLES

US #11/8mm needles for working flat
Or size needed to obtain gauge

NOTIONS

A single needle a size or two larger than the working needle, for binding off

US #G-6/4mm crochet hook

5 stitch markers

One 1-inch/2.5cm button

Yarn needle

GAUGE

12 sts/18 rows = 4 inches/10cm square in stockinette stitch

11 sts/19 rows = 4 inches/10cm square in seed stitch

SIZES

S (M, L)

stockinette stitch body. Increases are worked in six panels to create a rounded shape that skims the shoulders. The front and lower edges are also worked in seed stitch and the cape is fastened with a single button and a crochet chain button loop.

INSTRUCTIONS

COLLAR

Using the long-tail cast-on method, CO 49 (55, 61) sts.

Seed stitch all rows: K1, (p1, k1) to the end of the row.

Cont in seed st until the collar measures 5 (5, 5.5) inches/12.5 (12.5, 14) cm.

Inc row (WS): K1, p1, k1, m1, k10 (13, 13), m1, [k11 (12, 14), m1] 3 times, k1, p1, k1. 54 (60, 66) sts.

BODY

Row 1 (RS): K1, p1, k7 (8, 9), PM, [k9 (10, 11), PM] 4 times, k7 (8, 9), p1, k1.

Row 2 (WS): K1, p1, k1, p to last 3 sts, k1, p1, k1.

From here, the piece is worked with seed stitch at the edges as set, and stockinette stitch in the center.

SHAPE BODY

Inc row (RS): K1, p1, [k to 1 st before the marker, m1, k1, sm, k1, m1] 5 times, k to the last 2 sts, p1, k1. 10 sts increased.

Work 3 rows even.

Repeat the last 4 rows 3 (2, 3) more times, then work the inc row once more. 104 (100, 116) sts.

FOR SIZES M, L ONLY

Work 5 rows even.

Work the inc row again.

Rep the last 6 rows once more.

FINISHED MEASUREMENTS

Length from back of neck: 7 (8, 8.5) inches/ 18 (20.5, 21.5) cm

Neck circumference: 17.5 (19.5, 22) inches/ 44.5 (49.5, 56) cm

Width around shoulders at lower edge: 37 (43, 48.5) inches/94 (109, 123) cm

Measure around your neck just above your collarbone and choose the size that will fit most comfortably at this point.

PATTERN NOTES

Worked from the top down, the cape starts with the seed stitch collar, then transitions into the

FOR ALL SIZES

104 (120, 136) sts after incs are complete.

Next row (dec row, WS): K1, p1, k1, p48 (56, 64), p2tog, p to the last 3 sts, k1, p1, k1. 103 (119, 135) sts.

LOWER EDGING

Work 6 (8, 8) rows in seed st patt as given for collar.

Using the larger needle to work the stitches, bind off in pattern.

FINISHING

To block: Soak the piece with a wool wash if desired, press most of the moisture out, and use blocking mats and pins to gently shape. Leave it to dry.

Sew the button to the top of the seed st edge on the left side of the cape, just below the collar.

BUTTON LOOP

Using a crochet hook, chain 12. Fasten off.

Sew the button loop to the top of the seed st edge on the right side of the cape, just below the collar.

Fold the collar over onto the right side.

COSTUMING BY
Terry Dresbach

❧❧❧❧❧❧❧

In her three decades as an esteemed film and television costume designer, Terry Dresbach has sketched and designed clothing that's helped define the visual language of many memorable projects. But, arguably, she ended her career on a personal and professional high note with *Outlander*, the television adaptation of Diana Gabaldon's historical novels about time-traveling Claire Randall Fraser. A huge fan of the book series, Dresbach spent four seasons as the show's costume designer. She relocated to Scotland and from scratch built a costume shop and a network of local Scottish artisans to hand-make period-accurate costumes and textiles and source World War II–era military uniforms to tell the wardrobe story of eighteenth-century Scotland and twentieth-century America.

For every character, she meticulously researched the eras in which they resided and made sure their clothing choices were a reflection of both their inner and outer lives. Dresbach created mood boards and did deep research dives into the materials of the era to reproduce everything from Claire's wedding dress to young Brianna's '60s clothing and Jamie Fraser's Highland attire with the kind of accuracy few productions strive to attain. With her team of embroiderers, dyers, knitters, seamstresses, and tailors, Dresbach made it her personal hallmark to make sure the realities of the time were always mirrored in the clothing featured in every frame.

What the craftspeople created over four years now fills an entire costuming warehouse in Glasgow. And as a by-product, *Outlander* and Dresbach helped create the infrastructure for an expanded costuming industry to support the burgeoning film and television work in Scotland. For their labors of love on *Outlander*, the work by Dresbach and her team earned them two Emmy nominations and two Costume Designer Guild nominations. Dresbach retired from *Outlander* and costume designing in 2019 to spend more time with her family in California.

RENT
Shawl

Designed by Nicky Jensen

The inspiration for this pattern is the iconic shawl worn by Claire in episode 5 of season 1, when she travels with the rent-collecting party. This shawl has been knitted in bulky alpaca wool, to create a dense, soft, and warm layer, ideal for chasing Highland adventures.

At first glance this shawl looks like a perfectly plain, garter stitch triangle with two colored stripes. But look a little closer: the construction is very clever, and fun to knit, worked on the bias with intarsia. A simplified version of this pattern is provided, too, for a top-down triangular shawl with no short rows or intarsia required. The main difference visually will be that the rows will bias down instead of up.

SKILLS REQUIRED

Intarsia version: Intarsia, Kitchener stitch/ grafting

Simplified version: No special skills

MATERIALS

GGH Andania (100% alpaca; 54yds/49m per 1.75oz/50g ball)

Sample uses the following colors:

MC: color 11/Olive; 9 balls

CC1: color 12/Dark Green; 2 balls

CC2: color 15/Black; 2 balls

Substitution Notes: Desired yarn for this project is one with bulky weight in a natural animal fiber for its warmth and durability.

NEEDLES

US #9/5.5mm needles for working flat—a long circular needle is recommended

Or size needed to obtain gauge

NOTIONS

Stitch markers

Yarn needle

GAUGE

14 sts/18 rows = 4 inches/10cm square in stockinette stitch

15 sts/28 rows = 4 inches/10cm square in garter stitch

FINISHED MEASUREMENTS

Wingspan: 66 inches/167.5cm

Height: 33 inches/84cm

PATTERN NOTES

There are two versions of this pattern—one that sticks close to the construction of the one we see on-screen, and the other simpler and easier to knit. The original is constructed in a fascinating manner: it starts with a mitered square, the diagonal of the square reaching from the bottom tip up to the center of the neckline. As the shawl widens, stripes are worked with the intarsia technique. Once the full depth is reached, short rows are used to fill out one wing at a time, turning the square into a triangle. A garter edging finishes the top edge.

The simplified version is a standard top-down triangle shawl.

TECHNIQUES

- Intarsia is a technique that creates color blocks by working with multiple yarns in the same row. The non-working yarn is not carried but left hanging wherever it was last used, to be picked back up later on.
- To change from working with MC to CC1 using the intarsia technique: Working in garter stitch, both the RS and WS will be worked the same way

TIPS

- This pattern uses intarsia for the colorwork; this requires multiple working strands. The strands will get tangled and will have to be separated periodically. Some knitters choose to wind a bobbin for each strand and attach another length as needed to help minimize tangling. The trade-off is that this results in additional ends to weave in. Try using clips, such as large plastic hair clips, to temporarily secure balls of yarn to the fabric when they're not in use.

for a fabric that looks the same on both sides. Work all stitches of MC until a section of CC1 is reached. The strand will be hanging at the front of the work. Leave MC at the back of the work. Move CC1 to the back and under MC. Work all stitches of CC1. Do not carry MC. It will be right where you need it when you come back on the other side. Twisting the yarns together by passing one yarn under the other connects the two pieces of fabric.

MODIFICATIONS

This pattern can be easily modified to any size. While working the body, simply work until the spine measures half the desired wingspan, bearing in mind that size may increase somewhat with blocking. If you wish to wear it secured around the waist, as Claire sometimes does, be sure to take the wingspan measurement by placing the center of the measuring tape behind the neck, crossing the chest, and wrapping it around to the back of the waist.

INTARSIA SETUP PATTERN

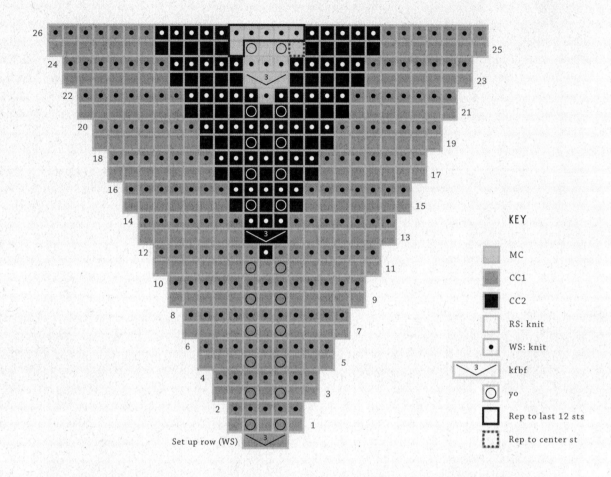

KEY

▨	MC
▨	CC1
■	CC2
☐	RS: knit
•	WS: knit
⌄3	kfbf
○	yo
☐	Rep to last 12 sts
⌐	Rep to center st

INTARSIA SETUP PATTERN

This is not used for the simplified version.

Work from the chart or the written instructions, whichever you prefer.

Setup row (WS): Kfbf. 3 sts.

Row 1 (RS): Pm between the first and second st to indicate the center st. Sl 1 purlwise wyif, knit to the center st, yo, sm, k1, yo, knit to the end. 2 sts increased.

Row 2 (WS): Sl 1 purlwise wyif, knit to the end.

Rows 3–10: Rep Rows 1–2 four more times. 13 sts.

Row 11: Rep Row 1 once more. 15 sts.

Add the second intarsia color:

Row 12 (WS): Sl 1 purlwise wyif, knit to the center st, attach CC2 and k1, attach a second strand of CC1 and knit to the end.

Row 13 (RS): Sl 1 purlwise wyif, with CC1 knit to the center st, with CC2 kfbf, with CC1 knit to the end. 17 sts.

Row 14: Sl 1 purlwise wyif, with CC1 k6, with CC2 knit to the last 7 sts, with CC1 knit to the end.

Row 15: Sl 1 purlwise wyif, with CC1 k6, with CC2 knit to the center st, yo, k1, yo, knit to the last 7 sts, with CC1 knit to the end. 19 sts.

Rows 16–21: Rep Rows 14–15 three more times. 25 sts.

Add the third intarsia color:

Row 22 (WS): Sl 1 purlwise wyif, with CC1 k6, with CC2 knit to the center st, attach MC and k1, attach a second strand of CC2 and knit to the last 7 sts, with CC1 knit to the end.

Row 23 (RS): Sl 1 purlwise wyif, with CC1 k6, with CC2 knit to the center st, with MC kfbf of the next st, with CC2 knit to the last 7 sts, with CC1 knit to the end. 27 sts.

Row 24: Sl 1 purlwise wyif, with CC1 k6, with CC2 k5, attach MC and k1, attach a second strand of CC2 and knit to the last 7 sts, with CC1 knit to the end.

Row 25: Sl 1 purlwise wyif, with CC1 k6, with CC2 k5, with MC knit to the center st, yo, k1, yo, knit to the last 12 sts, with CC2 knit to the last 7 sts, with CC1 knit to the end. 2 sts increased.

Row 26: Sl 1 purlwise wyif, with CC1 k6, with CC2 k5, with MC knit to the last 12 sts, slipping marker, with CC2 knit to the last 7 sts, with CC1 knit to the end.

~~~~~~

INSTRUCTIONS

Make a slip knot with CC1 and place on the needle. 1 st cast on.

Working from the chart or the written instructions, work Intarsia Setup Pattern, repeating Rows 25–26 until the spine measures approximately 30 inches/76cm (153 sts) or half the desired wingspan, bearing in mind that the size may increase with blocking.

RIGHT WING SHORT ROW SECTION

Cont working in the intarsia patt as set.

Short row 1 (RS): Sl 1 purlwise wyif, knit to the center st, w&t the center st. Mark the wrapped st with a st marker.

Short row 2 (WS): Knit to the end.

Short row 3: Sl 1 purlwise wyif, knit to 1 st before the marker, w&t the next st, moving the marker to the last wrapped st.

Short row 4: Rep Row 2.

Repeat Short Rows 3 and 4 to the end of the right wing sts. Remove the marker.

RIGHT WING GARTER EDGING

Cont working in the intarsia patt as set. Do not pick up wraps.

With the working yarn, CO 3 sts at the start of the row.

Row 1 (RS): K2, k2tog (1 st from the edging together with 1 st from the body), turn.

Row 2 (WS): Sl 1 purlwise wyif, knit to the end.

Row 3: Sl 1 purlwise wyif, k1, k2tog, turn.

Row 4: Rep Row 2.

Rep Rows 3 and 4 until the center st has been reached.

LEFT WING SHORT ROW SECTION

Cont with the working yarn in the intarsia patt as set.

Row 1 (RS): Sl 1 purlwise wyif, k1, k2tog. Knit to the end.

Row 2 (WS): Sl 1 purlwise wyif, knit to the last 3 sts, w&t the next st. Mark the wrapped st with the marker.

Row 3: Knit to the end.

Row 4: Sl 1 purlwise wyif, knit to 1 st before the marker, w&t the next st, moving the marker to the just-wrapped st.

Row 5: Rep Row 3.

Repeat Rows 4 and 5 until all the left wing body sts have been wrapped (except for the 2 edge sts).

RESUME GARTER EDGING

Cont working in the intarsia patt as set.

With the working yarn, CO 3 sts at the start of the row.

Row 1 (WS): K2, k2tog (1 st from the edging together with 1 st from the body), turn.

Row 2 (RS): Sl 1 purlwise wyif, knit to the end.

Row 3: Sl 1 purlwise wyif, k1, k2tog, turn.

Row 4: Rep Row 2.

Rep Rows 3 and 4 to the center st. 5 sts rem.

Next row (WS): Sl 1 wyif, k2. Break the yarn, leaving a generous tail and, using the yarn needle, graft the last 5 sts together using Kitchener stitch (3 sts on the front needle, 2 on the back).

SIMPLIFIED VERSION

GARTER TAB CAST-ON

In MC, CO 2 sts. Knit 6 rows. Turn the work 90 degrees and pick up 3 sts from the edge of the rectangle you have just knit. Turn the work 90 degrees again and pick up 2 sts from the cast-on edge. You will have 7 sts on the needle.

With RS facing, pm between the third and the fourth st to mark the center st.

Row 1 (RS): K2, yo, knit to the center st, yo, k1, sm, yo, knit to the last 2 sts, yo, k2. 4 sts increased.

Row 2 (WS): Knit across.

Rep Rows 1 and 2 until the center spine measures 29 inches/73.5cm, or 4 inches/10cm less than half the desired wingspan.

Change to CC2 and rep Rows 1 and 2 for 1.5 inches/4cm.

Change to CC1 and rep Rows 1 and 2 for 2.5 inches/6.5cm.

Bind off loosely.

FINISHING

Weave in the ends. To block: Soak the piece with a wool wash if desired, press most of the moisture out, use blocking mats and pins to stretch to desired measurements/shape, and leave to dry.

MRS. FITZ'S
Armwarmers

Designed by Barry Klein

Mrs. FitzGibbons is practical, and these are exactly the sort of thing you see her wearing as she bustles around the chilly castle, in the kitchen and elsewhere. Just like Mrs. Fitz, the yarn is warm but complex: the coloring is subtly shaded, with a little bit of cashmere to add softness.

SKILLS REQUIRED

Seaming, basic crochet stitches

MATERIALS

Trendsetter Yarn Basis (75% cotton, 16% brushed alpaca, 9% cashmere; 210 yds/192m per 1.75oz/50g skein); 2 (2, 3) skeins

Sample uses color 28844/White Blush.

Substitution Notes: Look for a yarn with a subtle color change to match the effect of the sample. For best stitch definition, choose a yarn with multiple plies, tightly twisted.

NEEDLES

US #3/3.25mm needles for working flat

Or size needed to obtain gauge

NOTIONS

Crochet hook in a size similar to the knitting needles

Yarn needle

GAUGE

24 sts/32 rows = 4 inches/10cm square in stockinette stitch

Approximately 36 sts/32 rows = 4 inches/10cm square in rib stitch, unstretched

SIZES

S (M, L)

FINISHED MEASUREMENTS

Circumference at hand: 7 (7.5, 8) inches/18 (19, 20.5) cm

Circumference at upper arm: 9 (9.5, 10.5) inches/23 (24, 26.5) cm

Length: 15 (15.5, 16) inches/38 (39.5, 40.5) cm

Note: Choose the size closest to your actual hand circumference, measured above the thumb.

PATTERN NOTES

Worked flat in a ribbing pattern, with the simplest of thumbs, these make an excellent project for an adventurous beginner knitter. Check the glossary for instructions for the m1 increase.

INSTRUCTIONS

Armwarmers are worked bottom up, from the hand toward the upper arm.

HAND

Using your preferred stretchy CO method—long tail or twisted German work well—cast on 61 (67, 73) sts.

SECTION 1

Row 1 (RS): K1, (p1, k1) to the end.

Row 2 (WS): P1, (k1, p1) to the end.

Rep Rows 1 and 2 three more times. 8 rows total.

Increase row (RS): K1, m1, (p1, k1) to the last 2 sts, p1, m1, k1. 2 sts increased.

Following row (WS): P2, (k1, p1) to the last st, p1.

Following row (RS): K2, (p1, k1) to the last st, k1.

Rep the last 2 rows twice more, and then work the WS row again. 7 rows total.

Next row, increase (RS): K1, m1, (k1, p1) to the last 2 sts, k1, m1, k1. 2 sts increased.

Following row (WS): P1, (k1, p1) to the end.

Following row (RS): K1, (p1, k1) to the end.

Rep the last 2 rows twice more, and then work the WS row again. 7 rows total.

SECTION 2

Row 1 (RS): K2, (p1, k1) to the last st, k1.

Row 2 (WS): P2, (k1, p1) to the last st, p1.

Rep Rows 1 and 2 three more times. 8 rows total.

Increase row (RS): K1, m1, (k1, p1) to the last 2 sts, k1, m1, k1. 2 sts increased.

Following row (WS): P1, (k1, p1) to the end.

Following row (RS): K1, (p1, k1) to the end.

Repeat the last 2 rows twice more, and then work the WS row again. 7 rows total.

Increase row (RS): K1, m1, (p1, k1) to the last 2 sts, p1, m1, k1. 2 sts increased.

Following row (WS): P2, (k1, p1) to the last st, p1.

Following row (RS): K2, (p1, k1) to the last st, k1.

Rep the last 2 rows twice more, and then work the WS row again. 7 rows total.

Work Sections 1, 2, and then 1 again. 81 (87, 93) sts. Continue even in rib pattern as required until the piece measures 15 (15.5, 16) inches/38 (39.5, 40.5) cm long, or desired length, ending with a WS row.

Bind off knitwise.

FINISHING

Soak in cool water and a wool wash if desired, press out excess water with a towel, and lay them flat to dry.

Starting at the bottom edge, sew the side seam closed, for 2.5 (3, 3) inches/6.5 (7.5, 7.5) cm. Carefully weave the yarn along 1 side edge up 1.5 (1.75, 2) inches/4 (4.5, 5) cm, to create the thumb opening. Continue sewing the side seam closed from this point up to the bound-off edge.

Historical Accuracy

⬚⬚⬚⬚⬚⬚⬚⬚

There's a lot of discussion about the *Outlander* costumes—lots of appreciation, of course, but also some debate. When working on a drama, costume designers have to strike a balance between historical accuracy and practical concerns, as well as considering visual appeal.

Historians know that there was indeed knitting in the eighteenth century, but it's highly unlikely the pieces on-screen are true to the period. The truth is, it's hard to be certain what is and isn't authentic. There's very little record of the sort of knitwear that ordinary people wore at that time, for the simple reason that very few pieces would have survived: although wool is hardy, knitwear is likely to have been worn to shreds, and any surviving items would have disintegrated over time. The other challenge, of course, is that, because of the oppression of the Scottish people and the suppression of their culture, there are few written records or images from the time.

TV costume designers work with modern materials and equipment, under very modern time constraints: the costumes for the entire first season were made in seven weeks, with a crew composed mostly of local craftspeople, using materials they could easily source. Creator Ronald D. Moore wanted to make them feel real, and as true to the period as possible within those constraints.

For obvious reasons, the most historically accurate pieces of knitwear in the show are from the twentieth century: Claire wears a gorgeous cabled pullover in her scenes in the 1940s, and a crocheted lace cardigan in the 1960s. Frank has a much-admired (and closely examined) Fair Isle vest, and Brianna wears a fantastic colorwork circular-yoke pullover in the 1960s. In all cases, these are items that were fashionable in their time, with patterns readily available. Our designers have done a wonderful job of creating homages to these garments.

DOUNE
Socks

Designed by Cheryl Eaton

Named after the historic Doune Castle, the inspiration for the design of these socks came from the eighteenth-century lace-up bodices, which are a feature of the dresses worn in *Outlander*. Overlapping diamond and textural cable motifs echo the crisscrossing shapes that are created by the bodice lacing. A hint of simple lace snakes its way through the diamonds, giving the socks a romantic, feminine feel. The Doune socks are worked in the round and are constructed from the top down with an eye of partridge heel flap, which adds strength and gives a very subtle lattice effect to the back of the heel.

SKILLS REQUIRED

Working small circumferences in the round on DPNs, with magic loop or with two circulars, working from charts, cables, lace, picking up stitches, Kitchener stitch/grafting (see page 182)

MATERIALS

GGH Elb Sox Heather (75% new wool, 25% polyamide; 230yds/210m per 1.75oz/50g ball); 2 balls

Sample uses color 549/Sand.

Substitution Notes: Choose a wool-and-nylon blend plied sock yarn with a high twist. A tightly spun yarn will help the cables to pop and will make your socks last longer.

NEEDLES

US #1/2.25mm needles for working small circumferences in the round (standard or flexible DPNs, 1 long circular or 2 short circulars)

Or size needed to obtain gauge

NOTIONS

Stitch markers

Cable needle (optional)

Yarn needle

GAUGE

38 sts/50 rounds = 4 inches/10cm square in stockinette stitch

40 sts/52 rounds = 4 inches/10cm square in pattern stitch

SIZES

XS (S, M, L, XL)

~~~~~~~~~~~~~~~~~~

FINISHED MEASUREMENTS

Foot/leg circumference: 7 (7.5, 8, 8.5, 9) inches/
18 (19, 20.5, 21.5, 23) cm

Choose a size approximately 1 to 1.5 inches/2.5 to
4cm smaller than your foot/ankle circumference,
measured around the ball of your foot.

~~~~~~~~~~~~~~~~~~

PATTERN NOTES

The socks start with my favorite long tail cast-on,
the twisted German or old Norwegian cast-on. This
gives a neat cast-on, which is nice and stretchy but
also durable—perfect for socks!

The cuff is then worked in a slightly offset rib,
which keeps the cuff section interesting. The ribbing
flows into the overlapping diamond cable and lace
motif against a reverse stockinette background. A
ribbon of textural twisted stitch panels borders the
diamond cables on each side. The diamond motifs
continue down onto the foot, ending in a completed
diamond before beginning the toe decreases.

The same motifs are repeated on the back of
the leg, before moving into an eye of partridge
heel flap.

MODIFICATIONS

For taller socks, extra repeats of Chart B can be
worked, but this will use more yarn than specified.

Extra repeats of Chart B can also be worked to
lengthen the foot before moving on to Chart C.

If the foot length is still too short after working
Chart C, continue to work rows 29–30 of Chart
C as many times as needed until the correct foot
length is achieved.

~~~~~~~~~~~~~~~~~~

CHARTS

SPECIAL STITCHES

1/1 LC: Slip the next stitch onto the cable needle
and place at the front of the work, k1, then k1
from the cable needle; (WS): Slip the next stitch
onto the cable needle and place at the front of the
work, p1, then p1 from the cable needle.

1/1 LPT: Slip the next stitch onto the cable needle
and place at the front of the work, p1, then k1 tbl
from the cable needle.

1/1 LT: Slip the next stitch onto the cable needle
and place at the front of the work, k1, then k1 tbl
from the cable needle.

1/1 RC: Slip the next stitch onto the cable needle
and place at the back of the work, k1, then k1 from
the cable needle. WS: Slip the next stitch onto the
cable needle and place at the back of the work, p1,
then p1 from the cable needle.

1/1 RPT: Slip the next stitch onto the cable needle
and place at the back of the work, k1 tbl, then p1
from the cable needle.

1/1 RT: Slip the next stitch onto the cable needle
and place at the back of the work, k1 tbl, then k1
from the cable needle.

KEY

☐	knit	⟍⟋	1/1 LC	⟍⟋	2/1 LT	▮	Size XS only
•	purl	⟋⟍	1/1 RC	⟋⟍	2/1 RT	▮	Size S only
Ⓠ	k tbl	⟍⟋	1/1 LT	⟍⟋	2/1 LPT	▮	Size M only
○	yo	⟋⟍	1/1 RT	⟋⟍	2/1 RPT	▮	Size L only
⟍	ssk	⟍⟋	1/1 LPT	⟍⟍	2/2 LT	▮	Size XL only
⟋	k2tog	⟋⟍	1/1 RPT	⟍⟍	2/2 LC		

CHART A (SIZES XS, S)

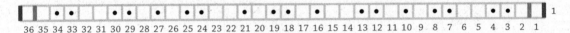

36 35 34 33 32 31 30 29 28 27 26 25 24 23 22 21 20 19 18 17 16 15 14 13 12 11 10 9 8 7 6 5 4 3 2 1 — 1

CHART A (SIZES M, L, XL)

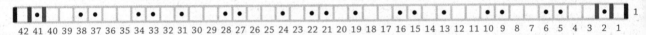

42 41 40 39 38 37 36 35 34 33 32 31 30 29 28 27 26 25 24 23 22 21 20 19 18 17 16 15 14 13 12 11 10 9 8 7 6 5 4 3 2 1 — 1

2/1 LT: Slip the next 2 stitches onto the cable needle and place at the front of the work, k1, then k2 tbl from the cable needle.

2/1 LPT: Slip the next 2 stitches onto the cable needle and place at the front of the work, p1, then k2 tbl from the cable needle.

2/1 RPT: Slip the next stitch onto the cable needle and place at the back of the work, k2 tbl, then p1 from the cable needle.

2/1 RT: Slip the next stitch onto the cable needle and place at the back of the work, k2 tbl, then k1 from the cable needle.

2/2 LC: Slip the next 2 stitches onto the cable needle and place at the front of the work, k2, then k2 from the cable needle.

2/2 LT: Slip the next 2 stitches onto the cable needle and place at the front of the work, k2 tbl, then k2 tbl from the cable needle.

INSTRUCTIONS

CUFF

CO 68 (72, 76, 80, 84) sts using the twisted German cast-on method. Distribute sts across the needles as you prefer and join for working in the round. Note or mark the start of the round.

Ribbing round: Working the chart for appropriate sizes, working sts as marked, work Chart A twice around.

Work in pattern as set until the cuff measures approximately 1.5 inches/4cm from the cast-on edge, or to desired length.

LEG

Leg round: Working the chart for appropriate size, working sts as marked, work Chart B twice around.

CHART B (SIZES XS, S)

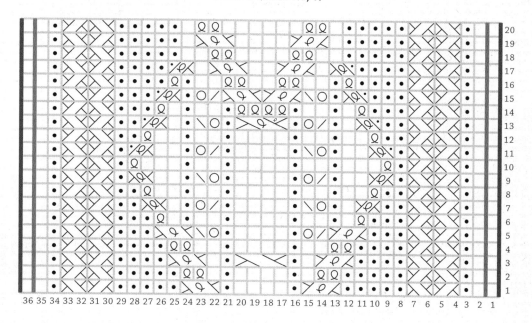

36 35 34 33 32 31 30 29 28 27 26 25 24 23 22 21 20 19 18 17 16 15 14 13 12 11 10 9 8 7 6 5 4 3 2 1

CHART B (SIZES M, L, XL)

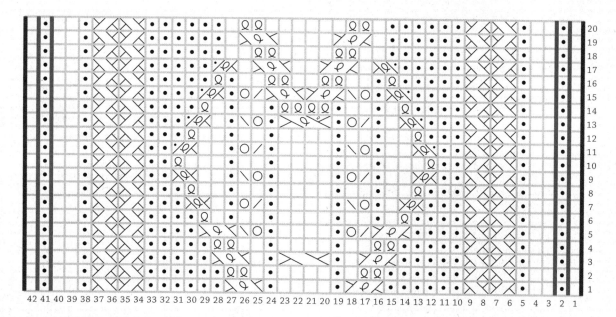

42 41 40 39 38 37 36 35 34 33 32 31 30 29 28 27 26 25 24 23 22 21 20 19 18 17 16 15 14 13 12 11 10 9 8 7 6 5 4 3 2 1

CHART C (SIZES XS, S)

Continue in pattern as set until you have completed all 20 rounds of the chart 3 times.

HEEL FLAP

Setup row: Work 34 (36, 38, 40, 42) sts in pattern as set, to the midpoint of the round. Leave these 34 (36, 38, 40, 42) sts on hold for the instep.

The heel flap will be worked back and forth across the second half of the round.

Row 1 (RS): Sl 1, p0 (0, 0, 0, 1), k0 (1, 1, 2, 2), p1, 1/1 RC, 1/1 LC, p1, (sl 1, k1) 10 (10, 11, 11, 11) times, p1, 1/1 RC, 1/1 LC, p1, k0 (1, 1, 2, 2), p0 (0, 0, 0, 1), k1.

Row 2 (WS): Sl 1, k0 (0, 0, 0, 1), p0 (1, 1, 2, 2), k1, 1/1 RC, 1/1 LC, k1, p to the last 7 (8, 8, 9, 10) sts, k1, 1/1 RC, 1/1 LC, k1, p0 (1, 1, 2, 2), k0 (0, 0, 0, 1), p1.

Row 3: Sl 1, p0 (0, 0, 0, 1), k0 (1, 1, 2, 2), p1, 1/1 RC, 1/1 LC, p1, (k1, sl 1) 10 (10, 11, 11, 11) times, p1, 1/1 RC, 1/1 LC, p1, k0 (1, 1, 2, 2), p0 (0, 0, 0, 1), k1.

Row 4: Sl 1, k0 (0, 0, 0, 1), p0 (1, 1, 2, 2), k1, 1/1 RC, 1/1 LC, k1, p to the last 7 (8, 8, 9, 10) sts, k1, 1/1 RC, 1/1 LC, k1, p0 (1, 1, 2, 2), k0 (0, 0, 0, 1), p1.

Repeat these 4 rows 8 (8, 9, 9, 10) more times.

CHART C (SIZES M, L, XL)

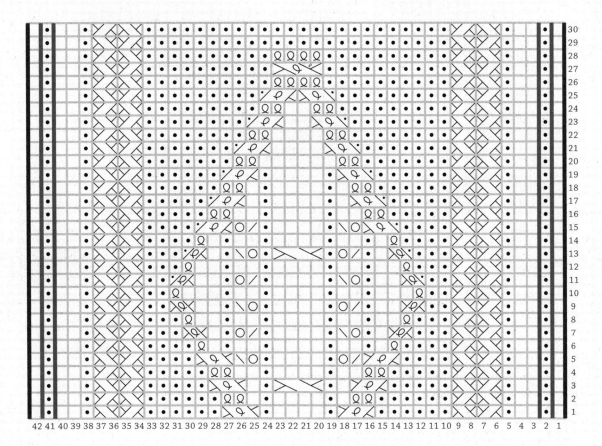

HEEL TURN

Row 1 (RS): Sl 1, k18 (20, 20, 22, 22), ssk, k1, turn.

Row 2 (WS): Sl 1 wyif, p5 (7, 5, 7, 5), p2tog, p1, turn.

Row 3: Sl 1, k to 1 st before the gap, ssk, k1, turn.

Row 4: Sl 1 wyif, p to 1 st before the gap, p2tog, p1, turn.

Repeat Rows 3–4 another 5 (5, 6, 6, 7) times until all the sts have been worked, ending after a WS row. 20 (22, 22, 24, 24) sts.

GUSSET

Setup round 1: Sl 1, k19 (21, 21, 23, 23) heel sts, then pick up and knit 18 (18, 20, 20, 22) sts along the side of the heel flap (1 st for every 2 rows worked), pick up and knit 1 st between the heel flap and the instep. Work across the instep in pattern as set. Pick up and k 1 st between the instep and the heel flap, then pick up and knit 18 (18, 20, 20, 22) sts along the side of the heel flap. K to the start of the instep. 92 (96, 102, 106, 112) total sts; 53 (55, 59, 61, 65) sts on sole; 39 (41, 43, 45, 47) sts on instep.

Round 1: Work across the instep in patt as set; k1, ssk, k to the last 3 sts of the sole, k2tog, k1. 2 sts decreased.

Round 2: Work even in patt as set.

Repeat Rounds 1–2 eleven (eleven, twelve, twelve, thirteen) more times. 68 (72, 76, 80, 84) sts rem.

FOOT

Work even in pattern as set. Each time you hit Row 20 of Chart B, measure the foot. You need to finish when the foot is no less than 3.5 (3.5, 3.75, 3.75, 3.75) inches/9 (9, 9.5, 9.5, 9.5) cm less than desired length from the back of the heel. Each repeat of Chart B will take about 1.5–1.75 inches/4–4.5cm. If you don't have enough space to work another repeat of Chart B before hitting that length, continue to the next section. You can make up any additional length after Chart C is complete.

Next round: Work in patt as set across the instep, working Round 1 of Chart C in place of Chart B.

Work as set until Chart C is complete. Repeat Rounds 29–30 of Chart C until until the foot measures 1.25 (1.25, 1.5, 1.5, 1.5) inches/3 (3, 4, 4, 4) cm less than the desired length from the back of the heel, ending on a Row 30.

TOE

Round 1: K1, ssk, k to the last 3 sts of the instep, k2tog, k2, ssk, k to the last 3 sts of the round, k2tog, k1. 4 sts decreased.

Round 2: K all sts.

Repeat Rounds 1–2 five (five, five, six, six) more times. 44 (48, 52, 52, 56) sts rem.

Work Round 1 five (six, seven, six, seven) more times. 24 (24, 24, 28, 28) sts rem.

Make sure that sts are divided evenly over 2 needles so that there are 12 (12, 12, 14, 14) sts each for the instep and the sole. Cut yarn, leaving a 12-inch (30cm) tail. Using Kitchener stitch, graft the toe closed.

FINISHING

Soak the socks for about 20 minutes in cool water with a dash of wool wash. Remove from the water and gently squeeze out the excess water. Lay the socks flat to dry. Weave in the ends.

RIVER RUN
Shawl

Designed by Eimear Earley

The River Run Shawl takes inspiration from the contrast of texture and fabric qualities of the red dress Claire wears during a visit to Jamie's aunt, Jocasta, at her home, River Run, in episode 2 of season 4. The dress is made of a sturdy woven fabric, with what appears to be a biased binding edging. Underneath the sleeve, Claire wears a ruffled, off-white, lace cuff, with floral motifs.

The shawl consists of a garter stitch crescent shape and a stockinette stitch welt border, both worked in DK weight yarn. The shawl is finished with a lace edging, worked in a delicate lace-weight yarn, with a simple motif that is reminiscent of flower petals.

SKILLS REQUIRED

Working from charts, lace

MATERIALS

MC: Trendsetter Yarns New York (100% pure organic wool; 190yds/174m per 1.75oz/50g skein); 3 skeins

Sample uses color SM036/Red Melange.

CC: Cardiff Cashmere Brushlight (82% cashmere, 18% silk; 150yds/137m per 0.88oz/25g skein); 2 skeins

Sample uses color 104/Pumice.

Substitution Notes: Trendsetter Yarns New York is a two-ply woolen-spun yarn of 100% wool, and is non-superwash. It is soft to touch, with some bounce, and feels slightly grippy. Cardiff Cashmere Brushlight is a lace-weight yarn with a soft halo, around a textured yarn core. The yarn is made of two different-size plies.

NEEDLES

US #6/4mm needles for working flat—a long circular needle is recommended

US #3/3mm needles for working flat

Or size needed to obtain gauge

NOTIONS

Stitch markers

Darning needle

Additional circular knitting needle, slightly smaller than the gauge needle (used to join the welt)

Optional crochet hook, to assist with nupps

Mats, towels, and pins for blocking

GAUGE

20 sts/28 rows = 4 inches/10cm square in stockinette stitch, worked flat using US #6/4mm needles (MC yarn)

18 sts/40 rows = 4 inches/10cm square in garter stitch, using US #6/4mm needles (MC yarn)

26 sts/38 rows = 4 inches/10cm square in stockinette stitch using US #3/3.25mm needles (CC yarn)

FINISHED MEASUREMENTS

Width: 65 inches/165cm

Depth at center: 17.5 inches/44.5cm

PATTERN NOTES

The River Run Shawl is a top-down crescent shawl, worked in a DK weight yarn, finished with a lace-weight edging. The shawl begins with a garter stitch tab, and is worked in garter stitch, with increases every row to form a crescent shape. The crescent is bordered with a welt worked in stockinette stitch. Then the yarn is changed to a delicate lace weight, and the simple lace edging is worked.

You can easily adjust the shawl for a different size or yarn quantity. Simply work the garter stitch crescent section to the size you wish, making sure that you end with a multiple of 12 sts plus 7.

RIVER RUN LACE PATTERN

Work from the chart or the written instructions, whichever you prefer.

RIVER RUN LACE PATTERN

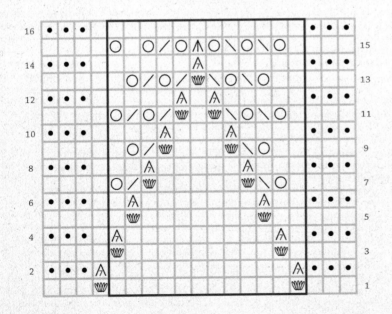

KEY

	RS: knit WS: purl
•	WS: knit
nupp symbol	nupp
Λ	p7tog
O	yo
/	k2tog
\	ssk
⋀	sl2tog, k1, p2sso
☐	12-stitch repeat

Row 1 (RS): K3, *nupp, k11, rep from * to the last 4 sts, nupp, k3.

Row 2 (WS): K3, p7tog, *p11, p7tog; rep from * to the last 3 sts, k3.

Row 3: K3, *k1, nupp, k9, nupp; rep from * to the last 4 sts, k4.

Row 4: K3, p1, *p7tog, p9, p7tog, p1; rep from * to the last 3 sts, k3.

Row 5: K3, *k2, nupp, k7, nupp, k1; rep from * to the last 4 sts, k4.

Row 6: K3, p1, *p1, p7tog, p7, p7tog, p2; rep from * to the last 3 sts, k3.

Row 7: K3, *k1, yo, ssk, nupp, k5, nupp, k2tog, yo; rep from * to the last 4 sts, k4.

Row 8: K3, p1, *p2, p7tog, p5, p7tog, p3; rep from * to the last 3 sts, k3.

Row 9: K3, *k2, yo, ssk, nupp, k3, nupp, k2tog, yo, k1; rep from * to the last 4 sts, k4.

Row 10: K3, p1, *(p3, p7tog) twice, p4; rep from * to the last 3 sts, k3.

Row 11: K3, *k1, (yo, ssk) twice, nupp, k1, nupp, (k2tog, yo) twice; rep from * to the last 4 sts, k4.

Row 12: K3, p1, *p4, p7tog, p1, p7tog, p5; rep from * to the last 3 sts, k3.

Row 13: K3, *k2, (yo, ssk) twice, nupp, (k2tog, yo) twice, k1; rep from * to the last 4 sts, k4.

Row 14: K3, p1, *p5, p7tog, p6; rep from * to the last 3 sts, k3.

Row 15: K3, *k1, (yo, ssk) twice, yo, sl 2, k1, p2sso, yo, k2tog, yo, k1, yo; rep from * to the last 4 sts, k4.

Row 16: K3, p to the last 3 sts, k3.

SPECIAL STITCHES

NUPP

This shawl uses a 7-stitch nupp. Into the next stitch, (k1, yo) 3 times, then k1 once more (increasing 1 to 7 stitches). On the WS row, these 7 stitches will be purled together. A crochet hook can assist with purling together the nupp stitches.

P7TOG

Purl the 7 stitches of the nupp together.

YARNOVER BIND-OFF METHOD

K1, *yo on the right needle, k1; lift both the yo and the right-most knit stitch over the stitch just worked; repeat from * until all stitches have been worked. Cut the yarn and pull through the final stitch to secure.

~~~~~~~~~~~~~~~~~~~~~~~~~~~~

INSTRUCTIONS

GARTER TAB

Using MC, CO 3 sts.

K 6 rows.

Turn the work 90 degrees, pick up and knit 3 sts along the side edge of the piece; turn the work 90 degrees and pick up and knit 3 sts in the CO edge. 9 sts.

Setup row: K3, pm, k3, pm, k3.

GARTER STITCH CRESCENT

Row 1 (WS): K3, sm, m1, k to marker, m1, sm, k3. 2 sts increased.

Repeat this row 142 times more. 295 sts. See Pattern Notes on page 48 about adjusting for different sizes or yarn quantities.

STOCKINETTE STITCH WELT

Row 1 (RS): Knit across, removing the markers as you encounter them.

Row 2 (WS): Purl.

Row 3: Knit.

Row 4: Purl.

Rows 5–6: Knit.

JOINING THE WELT

Turn so that the WS is facing. Using the smaller needle, and working from right to left, insert the needle tip into the upper purl bump of the first stitch of the first stockinette stitch row. Continue to pick up stitches along the back of this first row, until you have picked up 1 bump for every stitch. 295 picked-up sts.

Turn the work with RS facing, holding the live stitches parallel with the picked-up stitches.

*K 1 live stitch together with 1 picked-up st. Rep from * to the end of the row.

Break the MC yarn.

LACE SECTION

Join the CC yarn.

Row 1 (WS): K3, p to the last 3 sts, k3.

Row 2 (RS): Knit.

Row 3: K3, p to the last 3 sts, k3.

Next row: Work the River Run Lace pattern, working 12-st repeat as required.

Continue as set until the Lace pattern is complete.

With RS facing, using the yarnover bind-off method, bind off all stitches.

FINISHING

Weave in the ends. Soak in warm water with suitable wool wash or detergent, rinsing as required. Press between towels to remove the excess water.

Lay on a flat surface, gently smoothing out the garter stitch section. Pin along the top first, into a straight line, from the center outward. Continuing to smooth out the garter stitch, pin along the welt, working from the center out. Tease and stretch the lace out into shape, pinning out each point at stitches 4 and 16 from the chart.

Allow the piece to dry fully before removing the pins.

TARGE
Tam

Designed by Claire Neicho

A traditional round shield used by Scotsmen from the 1500s until the Battle of Culloden, the targe was an important item in the kit of a Highland warrior. Jamie can be seen charging into battle with a targe at the Battle of Prestonpans in episode 10 of season 2.

These shields were usually faced with leather, which was nailed to the wood with brass studs arranged in decorative patterns around a central emblem, and the leather was often embossed with Celtic patterns. Targes like Jamie's have served as the inspiration for the patterns used in the Targe Tam. The color palette for the tam comes from *Outlander*'s Fraser tartan, which incorporates earthy browns, neutrals, and grayish blues with accents of red and gold.

The tam is worked in the round, using the stranded colorwork technique. The body features a border pattern that evokes Celtic knotwork, with a traditional peerie pattern on either side. The seven-section wheel (crown) showcases patterns drawn from the decorative arrangement of the brass studs on targes.

SKILLS REQUIRED

Working small circumferences in the round on DPNs, with magic loop, or with two circulars; working from charts; stranded colorwork

MATERIALS

Jamieson & Smith's 2-Ply Jumper Weight (100% Shetland wool; 125yds/115m per 0.88oz/25g ball)

Sample uses the following colors:

MC: color 5; 1 ball

CC1: color 4; 1 ball

CC2: color 78 mix; 1 ball

CC3: color FC61 mix; 1 ball

CC4: color 2; 1 ball

CC5: color 202; 1 ball

CC6: color 1403; 1 ball

CC7: color 28; 1 ball

Note: The larger sizes use up almost a whole ball of MC. You will likely need to undo your swatch, or buy another ball as insurance.

Substitution Notes: A 100% wool yarn that has the capacity to felt is recommended. There should be sufficient contrast in color between MC/CC1/CC2 and CC3/CC4/CC5 as well as between MC and CC6/CC7 in order for the patterns to stand out from the background.

NEEDLES

US #2.5/3mm needles: 16-inch/40cm circular, 24-inch/60cm circular, and, for working small

SEASON 2
EPISODE 10

circumferences in the round, standard or flexible DPNs, 1 long circular or 2 short circulars

Or size needed to obtain gauge

NOTIONS

Stitch marker

Yarn needle

GAUGE

27 sts/36 rounds = 4 inches/10cm square in stockinette stitch

30 sts/36 rounds = 4 inches/10cm square in pattern stitch

SIZES

S (M, L)

FINISHED MEASUREMENTS

Circumference of brim: 18.5 (20, 22) inches/47 (51, 56) cm

Circumference of body of hat: 22.5 (24, 25.5) inches/57 (61, 65) cm

Height from bottom of brim to center of crown: 9.75 (10, 10.25) inches/25 (25.5, 26) cm

Note: Choose a size with a brim circumference that is 2 inches/5cm smaller than your head circumference, sizing down if you're in between sizes.

PATTERN NOTES

The tam is knitted in the round from the bottom up, using the stranded technique. The brim is worked in a two-color double rib, and the crown uses double decreases.

CHARTS

KEY

☐	knit
•	purl
⋀	sl2tog, k1, p2sso
■	MC
■	CC1
■	CC2
■	CC3
■	CC4
■	CC5
■	CC6
■	CC7

RIB CHART

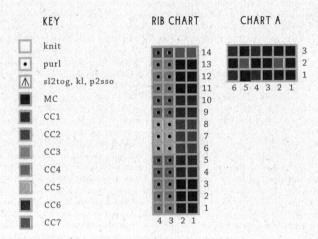

CHART A

CHART B

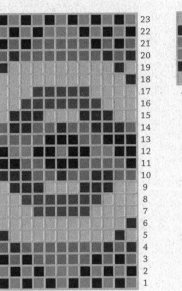

CHART C

CROWN CHART (SIZE M, L)

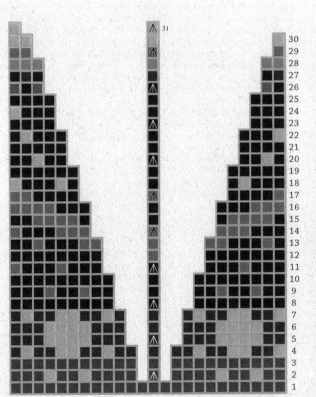

CROWN CHART (SIZE S)

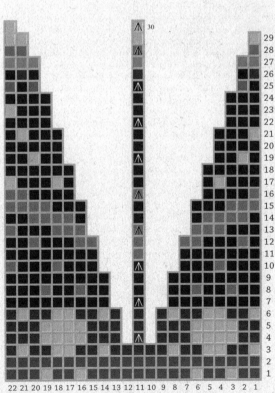

INSTRUCTIONS

BRIM

Using the shorter circular needle and CC6, cast on 140 (152, 168) sts. Place marker and join for working in the round.

Ribbing round: Work the Rib Chart 35 (38, 42) times around.

Joining colors as required, work as set until the chart is complete.

BODY OF HAT

Inc round: Using MC, [k8 (9, 14), m1] 4 (8, 12) times, [k9 (10, –) m1] 12 (8, –) times. 156 (168, 180) sts.

Change to the longer circular needle.

Using MC, knit 1 (2, 2) round(s).

Body round: Work Chart A 26 (28, 30) times around.

Work as set until Chart A is complete.

Using MC, knit 1 (1, 2) round(s).

Inc round: Using MC, [k13 (14, 15), m1] 12 (12, 12) times. 168 (180, 192) sts.

Next round: Work Chart B 14 (15, 16) times around.

Work as set until Chart B is complete.

Using MC, knit 1 (1, 2) round(s).

Dec round: Using MC [k12 (13, 14), k2tog)] 12 (12, 12) times. 156 (168, 180) sts.

Work Chart A in full again.

Using MC, knit 2 (3, 2) rounds.

FOR SIZE L ONLY

Dec round: Using MC, [k13, k2tog] 12 times. – (–, 168) sts.

> **TIPS**
> - To keep floats from becoming too tight, spread out stitches on the right-hand needle before changing colors.
> - To keep floats from becoming too long, weave in carried yarn halfway when knitting a run of more than five stitches in one color, staggering weaving-in points of subsequent rounds to minimize show-through.

FOR ALL SIZES

Next round: Work Chart C 39 (42, 42) times around. Work as set until Chart C is complete.

FOR SIZE S ONLY

Dec round: Using CC2, [k76, k2tog] 2 times. 154 (–, –) sts.

CROWN

Work the Crown Chart for your size 7 times around.

Work as set until the Crown Chart is complete. 14 sts rem.

Break the yarn, thread the tail onto the needle, and run it through the rem sts. Pull tight and fasten off.

FINISHING

Weave in the ends. Soak, with a wool wash if desired. Remove excess water by rolling in a towel and block over an upturned plate of a suitable size. You may find it helpful to place the upturned plate on top of a bowl (of smaller circumference than the plate) and to run a length of smooth waste yarn in long running stitches through the bottom of the ribbing, pulling tight around the bowl. Leave to dry before removing from the plate.

Fair Isle
KNITTING

Several projects in this book were inspired by the classic Scottish stranded colorwork technique known as "Fair Isle." The technique takes its name from one of the smallest Shetland Islands. Although it's not believed to have been invented there (it likely came from Scandinavia), the islanders developed an expertise in Fair Isle and their work became renowned around the world.

Strictly speaking, the name "Fair Isle" is properly associated with the specific colors, patterns, and methods that the Shetland knitters used—the more general term is "stranded colorwork." The technique was firmly established by the mid-nineteenth century, which is why we don't see any examples of this technique in *Outlander* costumes until the twentieth-century settings. In addition to its beauty, stranded colorwork offers a very practical benefit—warmth! Each row or round is worked with two colors, swapping every few stitches to make geometric patterns. The strand of unused-color yarn that sits in the back of the work forms a lining, doubling the thickness of the fabric and making it more windproof. It's ideal for hats and mittens, especially for windy and wet climates.

Part of the joy in this type of knitting is the cleverness of the color patterning. Even the most complex designs still only use two colors at a time. The Man I Left Behind Vest (page 103) is a great example of this work: it uses multiple colors in different combinations to create an overall color-blended effect. This vest is a classic piece of early-twentieth-century men's wear. The look became fashionable in 1921 with a portrait of Edward III, then Prince of Wales, nattily attired in his golfing gear, which included a gorgeous Fair Isle sweater. The Randall-Fraser Sweater (page 133) is a wonderful example of a more Scandinavian use of stranded colorwork.

The Lovat Mitts and Cowl (page 73) would be an excellent skill-builder if you're new to this type of knitting. Once you've tackled that, you'll be well-equipped for the other colorwork projects in this book.

SASSENACH
Capelet Cowl

Designed by Allison Thistlewood

Inspired by the cowl that Claire wore in episode 3 of season 1, this soft accessory is destined to keep you warm and cozy no matter which time line you find yourself in. Tug the cowl down over your shoulders and it becomes a cozy capelet. However you decide to wear it, you'll love how quickly this project knits up on 12mm needles. A bulky-weight yarn, held double, adds an extra snuggle factor. The sample uses up almost all of eight balls of GGH Andania, a luxuriously soft, 100 percent superfine alpaca. Why not treat yourself? You never know when you might unexpectedly travel through time.

SKILLS REQUIRED

Provisional cast-on, three-needle bind-off

MATERIALS

GGH Andania (100% superfine alpaca; 54yds/49m per 1.75oz/50g ball)

Sample uses the following colors:

MC: color 7/Dark Chocolate; 2 balls

CC1: color 10/Hemp; 2 balls

CC2: color 8/Ecru; 2 balls

CC3: color 21/Petrol; 2 balls

Substitution Notes: Look for a lofty, lightly plied, bulky-weight yarn in a luxury fiber such as alpaca or merino.

NEEDLES

12mm needles for working flat

A spare needle in a similar size

Or size needed to obtain gauge

NOTIONS

US #O/12mm crochet hook

Waste yarn in a similar gauge and different color from your project yarn

Yarn needle

GAUGE

9 sts/11 rows = 4 inches/10cm square in stockinette stitch, with yarn held double

8 sts/14 rows = 4 inches/10cm square in garter stitch, with yarn held double

to the next. Once the knitting is completed, the stitches from the provisional cast-on are picked up with a second set of needles. A three-needle bind-off is worked to seam the cowl together.

SPECIAL STITCHES

yb: yarn back

yf: yarn forward

INSTRUCTIONS

With waste yarn and the crochet hook, provisionally cast on 35 stitches.

Note: Yarn is held double throughout.

Row 1 (RS): Using MC held double, *k9, pm; repeat from * 2 more times, knit to the last st, yf, sl 1.

Row 2 (WS): *Knit to the marker, yf, sl 1, yb; repeat from * 2 more times, knit to the last st, yf, sl 1.

STRIPE 1

Row 3: Knit to the last stitch, slipping the markers when you come to them, yf, sl 1.

Row 4: Repeat Row 2.

Repeat Rows 3 and 4 five more times. There will be 7 garter ridges.

STRIPE 2

Drop 1 strand of MC and join 1 strand of CC1.

Repeat Rows 3 and 4 seven times.

STRIPE 3

Cut MC and join a second strand of CC1.

Repeat Rows 3 and 4 seven times.

STRIPE 4

Cut 1 strand of CC1 and join 1 strand of CC2.

Repeat Rows 3 and 4 seven times.

FINISHED MEASUREMENTS

Circumference: 32 inches/81.5cm

Depth: 19 inches/48.5cm

PATTERN NOTES

The cowl is worked flat in garter stitch with a provisional cast-on, and features columns of stitches that are slipped on the wrong side and knit on the right side. The first stitch of every row is knitted while the last stitch of every row is slipped purlwise with the yarn in front for a clean, neat edge that mimics the slipped-stitch columns in the cowl.

The yarn is held double throughout the cowl, with colors transitioning in wide striped bands from one

STRIPE 5

Cut CC1 and join a second strand of CC2.

Repeat Rows 3 and 4 seven times.

STRIPE 6

Cut 1 strand of CC2 and join 1 strand of CC3.

Repeat Rows 3 and 4 seven times.

STRIPE 7

Cut CC2 and join a second strand of CC3.

Repeat Rows 3 and 4 seven times.

STRIPE 8

Cut 1 strand of CC3 and join 1 strand of MC.

Repeat Rows 3 and 4 seven times.

JOINING THE ENDS OF THE COWL

Gently undo the provisional cast-on, slipping the live stitches onto the spare needle. Make sure there are 35 stitches from the provisional cast-on picked up on the second needle.

Fold the cowl in half with RS facing out and needles parallel to each other. BO loosely, using a three-needle bind-off.

FINISHING

Weave in the ends. Soak the piece, with a wool wash if desired, and lay it flat to dry, gently shaping as required.

CLAN MACKENZIE
Boot Socks

Designed by Sarah Lehto

Even though *Outlander* is loaded with highly visible hand-knitted items, the less-visible humble sock is a crucial element in cold weather, especially for fighters. The idea for these socks came from the kilt pin worn by the MacKenzie men, engraved with the motto *Luceo non uro* ("I shine not burn"). The medallion cable stitch is suitable for both men and women, and the extra-long cuff looks great peeking over a pair of boots for everyone to see.

The reinforced stockinette heel flap and French heel turn are in keeping with the techniques of the mid-1700s. Knit a pair for everyone in your clan.

SKILLS REQUIRED

Working small circumferences in the round on DPNs, with magic loop, or with two circulars; working from charts; cables; lace; picking up stitches; Kitchener stitch/grafting

MATERIALS

Lang Jawoll Superwash (75% wool, 25% nylon; 229yds/210m per 1.75oz/50g skein); 3 (3, 4, 4, 4) skeins

Note: Each skein comes with a 5-gram tube of reinforcement yarn tucked inside.

Sample uses color 8105.

Substitution Notes: For longevity, choose a wool-and-nylon blend, with a tight twist. A plainer color is better to show off the patterning. Avoid highly variegated yarns.

NEEDLES

US #1/2.25mm and US #1.5/2.5mm needles for working small circumferences in the round: traditional or flexible DPNs, 1 long circular, 2 short circulars

Or size needed to obtain gauge

NOTIONS

Stitch markers

Cable needle

Yarn needle

GAUGE

36 sts/48 rounds = 4 inches/10cm square in stockinette stitch

48 sts/48 rounds = 4 inches/10cm square in pattern stitch, unstretched

SIZES

XS (S, M, L, XL)

FINISHED MEASUREMENTS

Foot circumference: 6.5 (7.5, 8.5, 9.5, 10.5) inches/16.5 (19, 21.5, 24, 26.5) cm

Leg length (from cuff to start of heel flap): 9 (10, 10, 11, 12) inches/23 (25, 25, 28, 30) cm

Note: Choose a size about 0.75 to 1 inch/2 to 2.5cm smaller than your foot/ankle circumference, measured around the ball of your foot.

PATTERN NOTES

These socks are knitted top down, with a subtly shaped leg, featuring a stockinette heel flap and a French heel turn.

In addition to decreases, that shape of the calf is accommodated by using a larger needle size for the top portion of the sock. If you have particularly skinny calves, you may wish to use the smaller needles only throughout the entire sock.

If you wish to make the socks shorter, cast on one size smaller using the smaller needles. Work a shorter amount of ribbing before working the Decrease Chart, omitting the decreases as follows. Starting with a k round, work in garter st for 7 rounds, then work Rounds 1–8 of the Leg Chart and 1–4 once more in place of Rounds 8–20 of the

Decrease Chart. Follow this with 7 more rounds of garter st, starting with a k round to complete the cuff. Work fewer repeats of the Leg Chart before beginning the heel.

PATTERN STITCHES AND CHARTS

Work from the chart or the written instructions, whichever you prefer.

LEG PATTERN

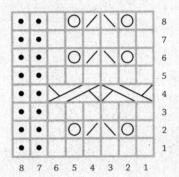

INSTEP PATTERN

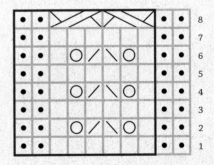

DECREASE CHART
(SIZES XS, L, XL)

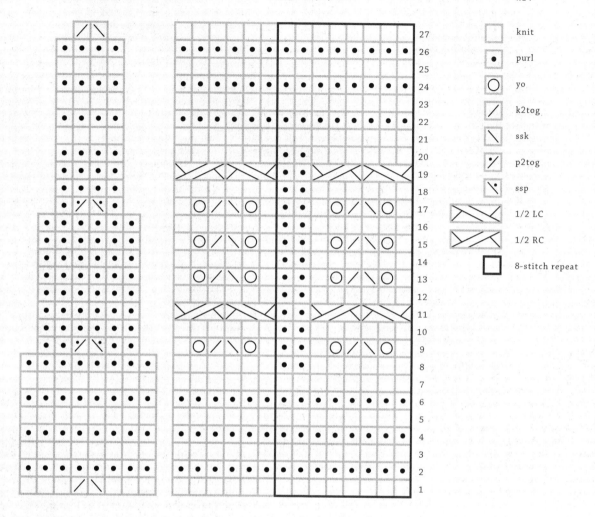

KEY

☐	knit
•	purl
○	yo
╱	k2tog
╲	ssk
⟋	p2tog
⟍	ssp
⤬	1/2 LC
⤬	1/2 RC
☐	8-stitch repeat

STITCH PATTERN FOR THE LEG

Round 1 (and all odd-numbered rounds): (K6, p2) to the end.

Round 2: (K1, yo, ssk, k2tog, yo, k1, p2) to the end.

Round 4: (1/2 LC, 1/2 RC, p2) to the end.

Rounds 6 and 8: Rep Round 2.

STITCH PATTERN FOR THE INSTEP

Round 1 (and all odd-numbered rounds): P2 (k6, p2) to the end of the instep.

Round 2: P2 (k1, yo, ssk, k2tog, yo, k1, p2) to the end of the instep.

Rounds 4 and 6: Rep Round 2.

Round 8: P2 (1/2 LC, 1/2 RC, p2) to the end of the instep.

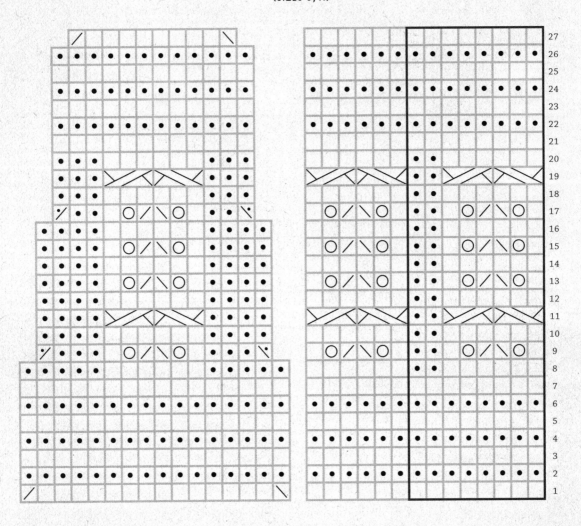

SPECIAL STITCHES

1/2 LC: Slip 1 st onto the cable needle, hold to the front, k2 sts, k st from the cable needle.

1/2 RC: Slip 2 sts onto the cable needle, hold to the back, k1, k sts from cable needle.

INSTRUCTIONS

CUFF

With the larger needles, and using the long-tail or another stretchy cast-on method of your choice, CO 72 (80, 88, 96, 104) sts. Distribute the sts across the needles as you prefer and join for working in the round. Note or mark the start of the round.

Ribbing round: (K2tbl, p2) to the end of the round.

Repeat ribbing round until work measures 2 inches/5cm.

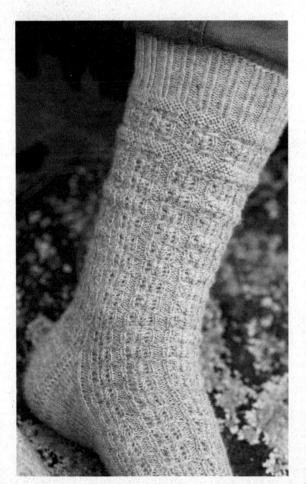

LEG DECREASES

Using the appropriate Decrease Chart for your size, decrease sts for the leg as follows:

Dec round: Work the appropriate Decrease Chart for your size, working an 8-st repeat 7 (7, 8, 10, 11) times.

When the chart is complete, 64 (72, 80, 88, 96) sts remain.

LEG

Leg round: Work the leg pattern around, working an 8-st repeat 8 (9, 10, 11, 12) times.

Cont until you have worked Rounds 1–8 of the leg pattern 3 times, then Rounds 1–3 once more.

The work measures approximately 6 inches/15cm from the cast-on edge.

Change to the smaller needles and cont in the leg pattern until the work measures approximately 9 (10, 10, 11, 12) inches/23 (25, 25, 28, 30) cm from the cast-on edge, ending with Round 4.

HEEL FLAP

Setup: K6, (p2, k6) 1 (1, 1, 2, 2) times.

The heel flap will now be worked in rows over the last 30 (38, 38, 46, 46) sts worked. Place the remaining 34 (34, 42, 42, 50) sts on hold for the instep. Turn so that the wrong side is facing. Pick up the reinforcement yarn and hold it together with the working yarn throughout the heel flap and heel turn.

Row 1 (WS): K3, p24 (32, 32, 40, 40), k3, turn.

Row 2 (RS): K30 (38, 38, 46, 46), turn.

Work Rows 1 and 2 for a total of 28 (30, 32, 34, 34) rows.

HEEL TURN

Row 1 (WS): Sl 1, p16 (20, 20, 24, 24), p2tog, p1, turn.

Row 2 (RS): Sl 1, k5, ssk, k1, turn.

Row 3: Sl 1, p to 1 st before the gap, p2tog, p1, turn.

Row 4: Sl 1, k to 1 st before the gap, ssk, k1, turn.

Repeat Rows 3 and 4 until all sts have been worked, ending with a RS row. 18 (22, 22, 26, 26) heel sts rem.

GUSSET

Resume working in the round as follows:

Break the reinforcement yarn and, with the main yarn only, pick up and knit 15 (16, 17, 18, 18) sts along the side of the heel flap (1 st in each garter ridge and 1 st to close up the gap between the heel and the instep); work Round 1 of the instep pattern over the 34 (34, 42, 42, 50) previously held instep sts, pick up and knit 15 (16,17, 18, 18) sts along the other side of the heel flap (1 st in each garter ridge and 1 st to close up the gap between the heel and the instep), k9 (11, 11, 13, 13) heel sts. This is the new beginning of round. Place a marker or rearrange the sts, whichever you prefer. 82 (88, 98, 104, 112) sts.

Round 1: K to the instep, work the instep pattern as set, k to the end of the round.

Round 2: K to 2 sts before the instep, k2tog, work the instep pattern as set, ssk, k to the end of the round. 2 sts decreased.

Repeat Rounds 1 and 2 until 64 (72, 80, 88, 96) sts rem.

FOOT

Work even in patt as set until the foot measures approximately 1.75 (2, 2, 2, 2.25) inches/4.5 (5, 5, 5, 5.5) cm less than desired foot length, ending with Round 4 of the instep pattern.

TOE

The toe will now be worked in stockinette st. Redistribute your sts so that you have 32 (36, 40, 44, 48) sts each for the sole and the instep.

Setup for toe: K to the new start of the instep.

Hold 1 strand of reinforcement yarn together with the working yarn for the entire toe.

Round 1: K to the end of the round.

Round 2: K1, ssk, k to 3 sts before the end of the instep, k2tog, k2, ssk, k to 3 sts before the end of the round, k2tog, k1. 4 sts decreased.

Repeat Rounds 1 and 2 seven (eight, nine, ten, eleven) more times, then work Round 1 only 3 (3, 4, 5, 5) times. 20 (24, 24, 24, 28) sts rem.

Using Kitchener stitch, graft the toe closed.

FINISHING

Soak the socks for about 20 minutes in cool water with a dash of wool wash. Remove from the water and gently squeeze out the excess water. Lay the socks flat to dry. Weave in the ends.

LOVAT
Mitts and Cowl

Designed by Karie Westermann

Inspired by Jamie's tartan with a pop of teal, the Lovat cowl and fingerless mitts take their design cues from traditional Scottish colorwork. The intricate colorplay of Fair Isle knitting has been simplified to make the Lovat set appealing to knitters eager to try their hand at one of the most famous Scottish styles. The Frasers of Lovat are a Highland clan strongly associated with the area around Inverness; this set could have easily been worn by clanswomen on a damp autumn's day in the Highlands.

Both the cowl and the fingerless mitts are worked in the round, and never use more than two colors per row, as per traditional Fair Isle techniques. Both are very simply constructed, with no shaping, making them an ideal project for beginners seeking to build their colorwork skills.

SKILLS REQUIRED

Stranded colorwork

MATERIALS

Trendsetter Yarns Wish (75% organic wool, 25% polyamide; 165yds/151m per 1.75oz/50g skein)

Sample uses the following colors:

MC: color 887/Coffee; 2 skeins

CC1: color 166/Teal; 1 skein

CC2: color 165/Pearl; 1 skein

Substitution Notes: Trendsetter Wish is a tweedy yarn with a muted, slightly felted feel. Its blend of organic wool and polyamide makes it soft, but durable. To substitute, look for a light-worsted wool or wool-blend yarn with a soft hand and a nubby appearance.

NEEDLES

The needles you use depend on the size you wish to make.

For size S: US #3/3.25mm needles and US #6/4mm needles

For size L: US #6/4mm needles and US #7/4.5mm needles

For the cowl: 16–20-inch/40–50cm circular needle

For the fingerless mittens: Needles for working small circumferences in the round (standard or flexible DPNs, 1 long circular or 2 short circulars)

Or size needed to obtain gauge

NOTIONS

Yarn needle

For mittens only: Waste yarn in a contrast color

For cowl only: Stitch marker

GAUGE

S: 22 sts/30 rounds = 4 inches/10cm square in stockinette stitch, using US #6/4mm needles

26 sts/34 rounds = 4 inches/10cm square in pattern stitch, using US #6/4mm needles

L: 20 sts/28 rounds = 4 inches/10cm square in stockinette stitch, using US #7/4.5mm needles

24 sts/32 rounds = 4 inches/10cm square in pattern stitch using US #7/4.5mm needles

SIZES

S (L)

FINISHED MEASUREMENTS

COWL

Circumference: 18 (19.5) inches/45.5 (49.5) cm

Height: 7.5 (7.75) inches/19 (19.5) cm

FINGERLESS MITTS

Circumference: 7.5 (8.25) inches/19 (21) cm

Length: 7.25 (7.5) inches/18.5 (19) cm

For the fingerless mitts, choose the size closest to your actual hand circumference, measured above the thumb.

PATTERN NOTES

Both the cowl and the fingerless mitts are worked in the round.

The fingerless mitts have an afterthought thumb construction, where you knit the stitches where you want your thumb, using waste yarn. The waste yarn is later unpicked, and you pick up the stitches to create your afterthought thumb. If you wish to knit wristwarmers, rather than fingerless mitts, skip the afterthought thumb instructions and continue in pattern.

Both the cowl and the fingerless mitts can be lengthened by working an additional repeat of the chart before continuing in pattern. Please note that you will need an extra skein of MC if you choose to do so.

CHART

PATTERN

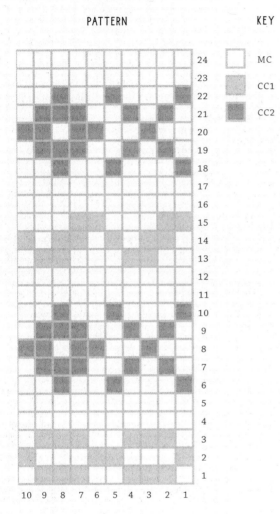

24
23
22
21
20
19
18
17
16
15
14
13
12
11
10
9
8
7
6
5
4
3
2
1

10 9 8 7 6 5 4 3 2 1

KEY

☐ MC

▨ CC1

■ CC2

INSTRUCTIONS

COWL

Using MC and smaller needle for your size, cast on 120 sts. Place marker and join for working in the round.

Ribbing round: (K1, p1) around.

Work 5 rounds of ribbing as set.

Change to larger needle.

Knit 1 round.

Joining CC1 and CC2 as required, work Rounds 1–24 of the chart twice, and work Rounds 1–5 once more.

Continuing to work in MC, change to smaller needle.

Work 5 rounds of ribbing as per lower edge. Bind off in pattern.

FINGERLESS MITTS

Using MC and smaller needles for your size, cast on 50 sts. Distribute sts across the needles as you prefer and join for working in the round.

Ribbing round: (K1, p1) around.

Work 10 rounds of ribbing as set.

Change to larger needles.

Knit 1 round.

Joining CC1 and CC2 as required, work Rounds 1–24 of the chart twice, and work Rounds 1–7 once more.

FOR THE LEFT-HAND MITT ONLY

Begin the afterthought thumb.

Round 8: Work the first 3 sts in pattern. Knit 8 sts using waste yarn. Slip these 8 sts back onto your left-hand needle and complete the round using the project yarn.

FOR THE RIGHT-HAND MITT ONLY

Begin the afterthought thumb.

Round 8: Work in pattern to 11 sts from the end. Knit 8 sts using waste yarn. Slip these 8 sts back onto your left-hand needle and complete the round using the project yarn.

SEASON
I
EPISODE
11

SEASON
I
EPISODE
10

FOR BOTH MITTS

Cont in patt as set until Round 17 of the chart is complete.

Continuing to work in MC, change to the smaller needles.

Work 5 rounds of ribbing, as per lower edge. Bind off in patt.

FOR THE THUMB

Remove the waste yarn, carefully returning the live sts above and below the gap to the needles—8 sts below, and 7 sts above, picking up a strand in each corner for a total of 17 sts.

Round 1: (K1, p1) to the last 3 sts, k1, p2tog. 16 sts.

Round 2: (K1, p1) around.

Work 4 rounds of ribbing, as per lower edge. Bind off in pattern.

FINISHING

Weave in the ends. Wash and lay the cowl and the fingerless mitts flat to dry.

SAUVEUSE DES ANGES
Capelet

Designed by Janelle Martin

This piece is inspired by the stunning mustard-colored cloak worn by Claire in episode 3 of season 2, and named for the hospital she visits. The lace patterns were selected based on the lace on the front of Annalise's gown, worn at Versailles in episode 2 of season 2. For a younger look that pays homage to kilts and aprons, the capelet can be worn over a short (or long) skirt, with knee-high boots, and fastened with a toggle closure.

SKILLS REQUIRED

Working from charts, lace

MATERIALS

Lana Grossa Alta Moda Cashmere 16 Fine (80% merino fine, 10% cashmere, 10% polyamide; 350 yds/320m per 1.75oz/50 g ball); 4 (4, 5, 5) balls
Sample uses color 35/Mustard.

Substitution Note: Look for a DK weight chained or constructed, non-superwash yarn with lots of loft, made with merino (with similar weight-to-length ratio). To come up with a similar look, select a heathered or tonal yarn to achieve a similar depth and stitch definition.

NEEDLES

US #6/4mm needles for working flat—a long circular is recommended

Or size needed to obtain gauge

NOTIONS

Stitch markers

Yarn needle

T-pins and flexible blocking wires (or your preferred tool for blocking on a curve)

Ribbon (7/8 inch/22mm wide) or closure to secure capelet at the neck

Sewing needle and matching thread

GAUGE

25.5 sts/40 rows = 4 inches/10cm square in stockinette stitch

23 sts/38 rows = 4 inches/10cm square in Chart B

SEASON
2
EPISODE
3

SEASON
2
EPISODE
2

81

SIZES

XS/S (M/L, XL/2XL, 3XL)

To fit bust up to: 34 (42, 50, 56 inches/86.5 (106.5, 127, 142) cm

FINISHED MEASUREMENTS

Width: 47 (51, 55, 58) inches/119.5 (129.5, 139.5, 147.5) cm

Length: 19 inches/48.5 cm

Use the "Modifications" information to choose a size. The capelet should be worn with several inches of ease.

PATTERN NOTES

Worked from the top down, the design begins with a stable edging of linen stitch and the linen stitch continues down the sides for a smooth edging. The shape is created using Elizabeth Zimmerman's Pi Shawl shaping between the lace patterns.

- For Chart A you will be working increases and decreases on both the RS and WS of the fabric. Please pay close attention to the stitch key, as different instructions are provided for the symbols, depending on whether you are working a RS or a WS row. It is strongly recommended that you place stitch markers between each repeat of the lace patterns; on Rows 1 and 4 you will need to remove the stitch markers to work decreases using stitches on both sides of the markers and replace them afterward.

MODIFICATIONS

To adjust for width (that is, larger bust sizes than given): Add stitches in multiples of 10 stitches. Each extra set of stitches will add 1 inch/2.5cm in width.

To adjust for length: Add repeats of Rows 5 to 24 of Chart C. Each repeat will add a little more than 2 inches/5cm in length.

CHARTS

CHART A

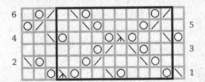

CHART C

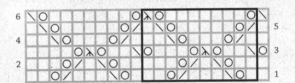

KEY

☐	RS: knit WS: purl
•	RS: purl WS: knit
○	yo
╱	RS: k2tog WS: p2tog
╲	RS: ssk WS: p2tog-tbl
⅄	RS: sl1, k2tog, psso WS: ssp-tbl-p2sso
⋀	RS: sl2tog, k1, p2sso
☐	Repeat

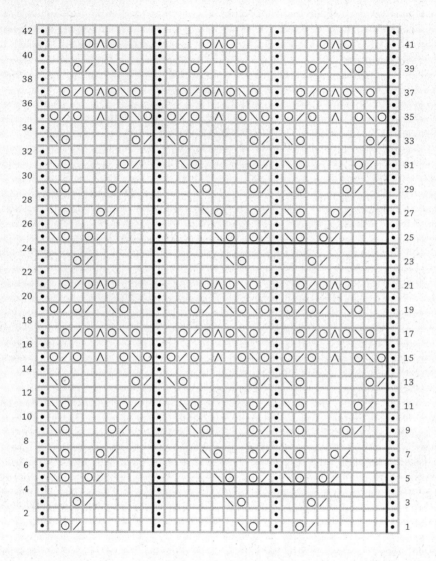

Inc row(WS): P1, sl 1 wyib, p1, m1, pfb 2 times, m1, (pfb 4 times, p1) 5 times, m1, pfb 20 times, m1, (pfb 4 times, p1) 5 times, m1, pfb 2 times, m1, sl 1 wyib, p1, sl 1 wyib. 150 sts.

FOR SIZE M/L

Inc row (WS): P1, sl 1 wyib, p2, m1, (pfb 7 times, p1) 12 times, p1, m1, sl 1 wyib, p1, sl 1 wyib. 190 sts.

FOR SIZE XL/2XL

Inc row (RS): P1, sl 1 wyib, p1, m1, pfb 37 times, m1, pfb 36 times, m1, pfb 37 times, m1, sl 1 wyib, p1, sl 1 wyib. 230 sts.

FOR SIZE 3X

Inc row (RS): P1, sl 1 wyib, p1, m1, pfb 15 times, m1, (pfb 13 times, m1) 7 times, pfb 16 times, m1, sl 1 wyib, p1, sl 1 wyib. 260 sts.

BODY

Continuing in pattern as set for the linen stitch edgings, begin working from Chart A as follows:

Row 1 (RS): K1, sl 1 wyif, k1, row 1 of Chart A working the 10-st repeat 14 (18, 22, 25) times, sl 1 wyif, k1, sl 1wyif.

Cont working from the chart as set and work through Chart A 7 times total, then work Rows 1–5 again.

FOR SIZE XS/S

Inc row (WS): P1, sl 1 wyib, p1, m1, pfb 72 times, m1, pfb 72 times, m1, sl 1 wyib, p1, sl 1 wyib. 297 sts.

FOR SIZE M/L

Inc row (WS): P1, sl 1 wyib, p1, m1, pfb 92 times, m1, pfb 92 times, m1, sl 1 wyib, p1, sl 1 wyib. 377 sts.

INSTRUCTIONS

INITIAL EDGING

Using a stretchy cast-on, such as the twisted German cast-on, CO 80 (104, 116, 128) stitches. Begin working the linen stitch edging as follows:

Row 1 (RS): (K1, sl 1 wyif) to the end of the row.

Row 2 (WS): (P1, sl 1 wyib) to the end of the row.

Work these 2 rows 7 more times, then work Row 1 once more.

Note: From this point on, a 3-st linen stitch edging will be continued at the beginning and end of every row. Increases will not be worked in this edging.

FOR SIZE XL/2XL

Inc row (RS): P1, sl 1 wyib, p1, m1, pfb 112 times, m1, pfb 112 times, m1, sl 1 wyib, p1, sl 1 wyib. 457 sts.

FOR SIZE 3XL

Inc row (RS): P1, sl 1 wyib, p1, m1, pfb 127 times, m1, pfb 127 times, m1, sl 1 wyib, p1, sl 1 wyib. 517 sts.

Cont in patt as set for the linen stitch edgings. Begin working from Chart B as follows:

Row 1 (RS): K1, sl 1 wyif, k1, row 1 of Chart B working the 20-st repeat 14 (18, 22, 25) times, sl 1 wyif, k1, sl 1 wyif.

Cont in patt, working from Chart B as set and work:

Rows 1–4 once.

Rows 5–24 four times total.

Rows 25–42 once.

BORDER

Cont in patt as set for the linen stitch edgings. Begin working from Chart C as follows:

Row 1 (RS): K1, sl 1 wyif, k1, row 1 of Chart C, working the 10-st repeat 28 (36, 44, 50) times, sl 1 wyif, k1, sl 1 wyif.

Cont in patt, working from the chart as set, and work through Chart C twice. Work Rows 1–3 once more. With WS facing, BO loosely using the modified Icelandic bind-off or another stretchy bind-off.

FINISHING

To block: Soak the piece with a wool wash if desired, press most of the moisture out, and use blocking mats, wires, and pins to shape. Leave it to dry.

Weave in the ends.

If you are attaching ribbons as a closure, stitch the folded-over end of the ribbon inconspicuously to the WS at the neckline (so the ribbon doesn't unravel).

LACE
Fichu

Designed by Maya Bosworth

Inspired by the little pieces of lace that appeared here and there in season 1, this design combines the fragile delicacy of lace with the unfussy, practical charm of the garter stitch knitwear of some of the costume pieces. It's fancy but still rugged enough to transport the wearer to the sometimes-harsh Scottish Highlands.

SKILLS REQUIRED

Working from charts, lace

MATERIALS

GGH Merino Melange (100% virgin wool; 186yds/170m per 1.75oz/50g ball); 6 balls
Sample uses color 3/Beige.

Substitution Notes: A lace-weight fingering yarn with a little bit of halo brings a rustic look. Yarn weight is not crucial—if you're working with a different weight, choose needles three or four sizes larger than recommended for the yarn, to create an open and delicate fabric.

NEEDLES

US #2.5/3mm needles for working flat—a long circular needle is recommended

Or size needed to obtain gauge

NOTIONS

Stitch markers

Yarn needle

Mats, wires, pins for blocking

GAUGE

27 sts/36 rows = 4 inches/10cm square in stockinette stitch

SIZE

One size

FINISHED MEASUREMENTS

Wingspan: 72 inches/183cm

Depth: 19.5 inches/49.5cm

PATTERN NOTES

This garter stitch crescent shawl is knitted from the top down, using a simple lace pattern throughout and finishing with a picot bind-off. All shaping is done at the edges. It is suitable for experienced knitters who are familiar with "filling in" with stitch patterns. However, the stitch pattern is simple, as is the crescent shaping, so the pattern could be suitable for confident knitters with a little lace experience who are looking to advance their skill level.

LACE PATTERN

BASIC LACE CHART

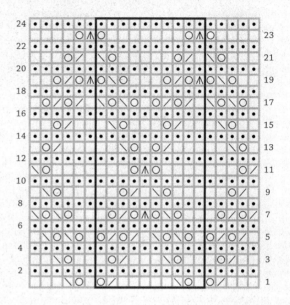

STARTING LACE CHART

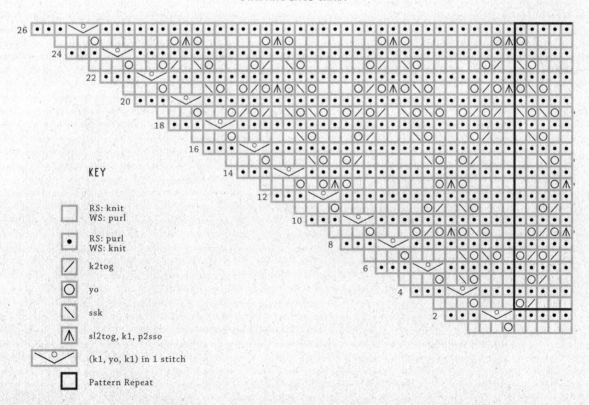

KEY

☐	RS: knit WS: purl
•	RS: purl WS: knit
╱	k2tog
○	yo
╲	ssk
⋀	sl2tog, k1, p2sso
⌣	(k1, yo, k1) in 1 stitch
☐	Pattern Repeat

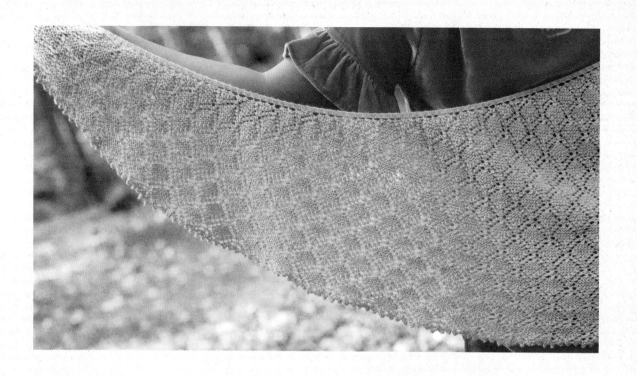

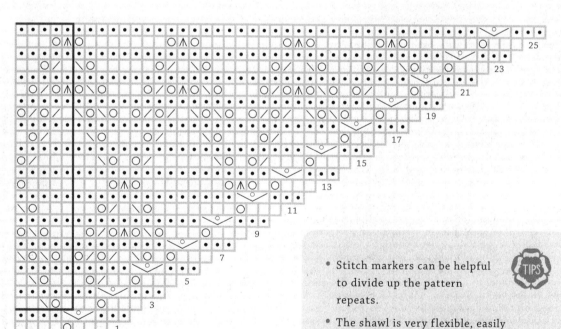

- Stitch markers can be helpful to divide up the pattern repeats.

- The shawl is very flexible, easily adapted to more or less yarn. Just keep working until you've almost finished the yarn you have.

INSTRUCTIONS

GARTER TAB

Cast on 3 sts and knit 5 rows. Turn the work 90 degrees to the right and pick up and knit 3 sts along the side of the garter strip; turn the work another 90 degrees and pick up and knit 3 sts in the cast-on edge. 9 sts.

BODY

Row 1 (RS): K3, pm, yo, k3, yo, pm, k3. 11 sts.

Row 2 (WS): K3, (k1, yo, k1) into the yo from the previous row, k3, (k1, yo, k1) into the yo from the previous row, k3. 15 sts.

Next row: Work from the Starting Lace Chart.

Work as set until the chart is complete.

At this point, you'll continue, working the increases as set:

RS rows: K3, yo, work in pattern as set to the last 3 sts, yo, k3. 2 sts increased.

WS rows: K3, (yo, k1, yo) into the yo from the previous row, k to the last 4 sts, (k1, yo, k1) into the yo from the previous row, k3. 4 sts increased.

As you're doing this, you will "fill in" additional repeats of the lace pattern, in the increased stitches. Once you've got 5 plain stitches between the first edge and the next lace motif, you can start working the plain stitches as per the first part of the Basic Lace Chart (page 88); and at the end work the last 6 stitches of the lace repeat. Once you have 10 stitches at the start, you'll have enough for a full lace motif. It doesn't matter what row you're on when you start the new lace motif. It's actually fairly forgiving: work as many stitches in lace as you can. Just remember, for every yarnover you add, there must be an accompanying decrease; for every decrease, there must be a corresponding yarnover. If there aren't enough stitches for the yo, CDD, yo, just work the yo and a single decrease.

Work in pattern as set until you've just about run out of yarn, ending with Row 12 or 24 of the basic pattern. You need about 10 times the width of the row in yarn to bind off. If you have a digital scale, weigh the yarn as you go to make sure you have enough.

WORK THE PICOT BIND-OFF AS FOLLOWS

*Using the knit method, CO 2 sts onto the left-hand needle. Bind off 4 sts. Slip the st back onto the left-hand needle and repeat from * until all the sts are bound off. You may need to fudge the stitch count as you get to the end of the row. You need to have 3 sts on the left-hand needle to work a complete picot—including the st that is slipped back. If you only have 1 or 2 at the end, work the cast-on as usual, and just bind off until no stitches remain.

FINISHING

Weave in the yarn tails and block gently. As this is a superwash yarn, just pop the shawl in the washing machine (avoid washing it with items that have zippers and other attachments, which may damage the shawl). Stretch the piece out to open up the lace, and pin to dry.

SEASON
1

EPISODE
12

91

PARIS
Connections

Designed by Mary Hull

In season 2, Claire and Jamie travel to Paris and rely on Jamie's old family connections to forge new ones with Charles Stewart in an attempt to prevent the Battle of Culloden. Claire's wardrobe rises to the level of those Paris connections and includes a stunning yellow dress she wears to drink tea—and gossip—with Louise and Mary. These fingerless gauntlets echo the bodice's detailed elegance.

They are worked from the cuff up, first in the round, then flat using intarsia, and are later seamed for easier colorwork yarn management. Choose colors true to the dress that inspired this project or pick different ones that resonate with you. With six sizes, you're sure to find one that fits, well, like a glove!

SKILLS REQUIRED

Working small circumferences in the round on DPNs, with magic loop, or with two circulars; working from charts; stranded colorwork; intarsia; seaming

MATERIALS

Sun Valley Fibers MCS-Fingering (75% merino, 15% cashmere, 10% silk; 400yds/366m per 3.5oz/100g skein)

Sample uses the following color:

MC: color Colonel Mustard; 1 skein

Sun Valley Fibers MCS-Fingering Mini-Skein (75% merino, 15% cashmere, 10% silk; 50yds/46m per 0.44oz/12.5g skein)

Sample uses the following color:

CC1: color Antler; 1 mini-skein

Sun Valley Fibers MCN-Fingering (80% merino, 10% cashmere, 10% nylon; 50yds/46m per 0.44oz/12.5g skein)

Sample uses the following color:

CC2: color Onyx; 1 mini-skein

Substitution Notes: Look for a fingering-weight wool blend. The cashmere adds a bit of luxury for your hands, while the silk content evokes the sheen of the Paris-season costumes.

NEEDLES

US #1/2.25mm needles for working flat, and for working small circumferences in the round (standard or flexible DPNs, 1 long circular or 2 short circulars)

Or size needed to obtain gauge

NOTIONS

Stitch markers

Stitch holders or scrap yarn for thumb stitches

Yarn needle

GAUGE

32 sts/44 rounds = 4 inches/10cm square in stockinette stitch

SIZES

XXS (XS, S, M, L, XL)

FINISHED MEASUREMENTS

Hand Circumference: 6.5 (7, 7.5, 8, 8.5, 9) inches/16.5 (18, 19, 20.5, 21.5, 23) cm

Hand Length: 7.75 (8, 8.5, 9, 9.25, 9.5) inches/19.5 (20.5, 21.5, 23, 23.5, 24) cm

Note: Choose a size with a circumference that measures 0.5 to 1 inch/13mm to 2.5cm less than actual hand circumference, measured above the thumb.

PATTERN NOTES

Like Parisian couture, some aspects of knitting this pattern can be a bit fussy, but with six possible sizes, you will be sure to find that custom fit. Start off by casting on and joining in the round to work the ribbed cuff from the bottom to the base of the hand. Transition to knitting flat—the center motif is charted with irregular placement of contrasting star stitches, inspired by the organic floral print on Claire's yellow dress, rather than a geometric repeating pattern. The chart is a mini-section of stranded colorwork where you may have to occasionally catch long floats on the wrong side. However, the chart links to the rest of the hand using intarsia—make sure to twist the working yarns every time you come to that join. Once the chart is complete for the chosen size, cut the contrast colors and rejoin for working the top ribbing in the round in the main color. At the end, close up the gap created by working flat with a tidy mattress stitch. Finish up with the thumb, and your Parisian couture piece is complete!

CHARTS

LEFT HAND
PATTERN

KEY

	CC1
	CC2
V	WS: slip purlwise with yarn in front
V Q	WS: kfb
K	RS: M1R
Y	RS: M1L
✳	Star
▮	End after Row 39 (43, 47, 51, 55, 59), based on your size

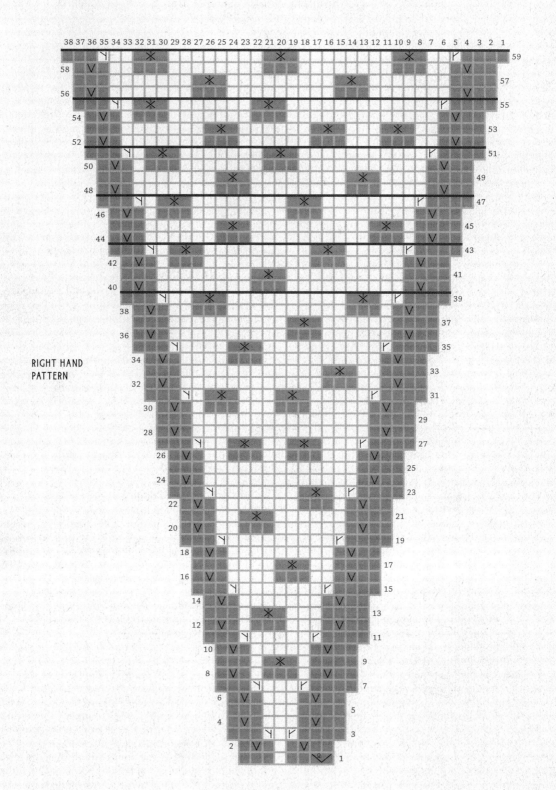

RIGHT HAND
PATTERN

INSTRUCTIONS

CUFF (BOTH HANDS)

With MC, CO 52 (56, 60, 64, 68, 72) sts. Distribute sts across the needles as you prefer and join for working in the round. Note or mark the start of the round.

Ribbing round: (K2, p2) around.

Work ribbing as set until the cuff measures 3.75 inches/9.5cm or desired length.

Next round: Knit.

HAND (KNIT FLAT: TURN AFTER EACH ROW)

Note: Make sure you follow the correct chart for each hand. The chart portion is worked in stockinette stitch in CC1 and CC2; the remaining sts are worked in MC. When you transition from the charted section to the MC section, twist the 2 yarns around each other to ensure that there are no holes.

FOR RIGHT HAND ONLY

Row 1 (RS): Work the Right Hand Chart with CC1 and CC2, pm for the end of the chart, with MC, k10 (11, 12, 13, 14, 15), pm for the thumb, M1L, pm for the thumb, k to the last st, kfb. 54 (58, 62, 66, 70, 74) sts.

FOR LEFT HAND ONLY

Row 1 (RS): Work the Left Hand Chart with CC1 and CC2, pm, k36 (39, 42, 45, 48, 51), pm for the thumb, M1L, pm for the thumb, k to the last st, kfb. 54 (58, 62, 66, 70, 74) sts.

FOR BOTH HANDS

The remaining instructions apply to both hands—make sure you are following the correct chart for the hand you are knitting, right or left. You'll be working increases for the thumb between the markers. As the charted area widens, you'll work decreases in the plain section of the hand.

Row 2 (WS): With MC, p across to the chart marker, continue the chart with CC1 and CC2. 55 (59, 63, 67, 71, 75) sts.

Row 3: Continue the chart with CC1 and CC2, slip the chart marker, ssk, k to the first thumb marker, sm, M1R, k to the second thumb marker, M1L, sm, k to last 3 sts, k2tog, k1. 2 sts increased for the thumb.

Rows 4 and 6: With MC, p across to the chart marker, continue the chart with CC1 and CC2.

Row 5: Continue the chart with CC1 and CC2, k to the first thumb marker, sm, M1R, k to the second thumb marker, M1L, sm, k to the end. 2 sts increased for the thumb.

Repeat Rows 3–6 until there are 21 (21, 23, 23, 25, 25) thumb sts, ending with Row 4 for sizes S and M and ending with Row 6 for sizes XXS, XS, L, XL. 75 (79, 85, 89, 95, 99) sts.

FOR SIZES XXS, XS, L, XL ONLY

Row 7: Cont the chart with CC1 and CC2, ssk, k to the last 3 sts, k2tog, k1.

Rows 8 and 10: With MC, p across to the chart marker, cont the chart with CC1 and CC2.

Row 9: Cont the chart with CC1 and CC2, k to the end.

FOR SIZES S, M ONLY

Row 7: Cont the chart with CC1 and CC2, k to the end.

Row 8: With MC, p across to the chart marker, cont the chart with CC1 and CC2.

SET-ASIDE THUMB (WORKED FLAT: TURN AFTER EACH ROW)

Row 1 (RS): Cont the chart with CC1 and CC2, ssk, k to st marker, remove the first thumb marker, place the next 21 (21, 23, 23, 25, 25) thumb sts on the holder and set aside. CO 1 st using the backwards loop method, remove the second thumb marker, k to the last 3 sts, k2tog, k1. 55 (59, 63, 67, 71, 75) sts.

Rows 2 and 4 (WS): P to marker, sm, cont the chart with CC1 and CC2.

Row 3: Cont the chart with CC1 and CC2, k to the end.

Row 5: Cont the chart with CC1 and CC2, ssk, k to the last 3 sts, k2tog, k1.

Repeat Rows 2–5 until Row 39 (43, 47, 51, 55, 59) of the chart is complete.

Next row (WS): P with MC to marker, rm, p1 with CC2, sl 1 wyif with CC2, p1 with CC2, p21 (23, 25, 27, 29, 31) with CC1, p1 with CC2, sl 1 wyif with CC2, p2 with CC2.

Cut all the yarns, leaving an 8-inch/20.5cm tail of MC and CC1 and a 30-inch/76cm tail of CC2.

TOP RIBBING (WORKED IN THE ROUND)

Row 1: K with MC to the last st. Rejoin for working in the round by knitting the last st together with the first st of the row. This is the new start of the round. 54 (58, 62, 66, 70, 74) sts.

Round 2: *(K1, p1) 5 (5, 6, 6, 7, 7) times, k2tog, p1, repeat from * 3 more times, (k1, p1) to the end. 50 (54, 58, 62, 66, 70) sts.

Rounds 3–5: (K1, p1) around.

Bind off all sts in the rib pattern.

THUMB (WORKED IN THE ROUND)

Place 21 (21, 23, 23, 25, 25) held sts back onto the needles for working in the round. With MC, k all sts, then pick up and knit 3 sts in the gap between the thumb and the hand. This is the new beginning of the round. 24 (24, 26, 26, 28, 28) sts.

Rounds 1–2: K around.

Round 3: K to the last 4 sts, k2tog, ssk. 22 (22, 24, 24, 26, 26) sts.

Knit around until the thumb is 0.5 inch/13mm less than the total desired length.

Round 1: *K9 (9, 10, 10, 11, 11), k2tog, repeat from * once more. 20 (20, 22, 22, 24, 24) sts.

Rounds 2–5: (K1, p1) around.

Bind off all sts in the rib pattern.

FINISHING

Soak the gauntlets in cool water and a wool wash if desired, press out excess water with a towel (do not wring!), and lay them flat to dry.

Using the long CC2 tail, mattress-stitch the open seam along the chart motif, sewing the horizontal bars just inside the edge sts. (This will eat up a st along either edge.) Weave in all the ends and cut the tails.

THE MAN I LEFT BEHIND
Vest

Designed by Kathleen Sperling

In the first season of *Outlander*, at the end of "The Way Out," Claire is despairing of ever returning to her own time. But then one evening, she hears a song performed in Colum's hall. The lyrics, translated to her by Jamie, tell the story of a woman who had an experience just like hers—by touching the tallest stone of Craigh na Dun, she had "traveled to a far, distant land, where [she] lived for a time among strangers who became lovers and friends." The song goes on to tell the second part of the woman's tale, where she touched the stone again and returned home, and "took up again with the man [she] had left behind."

After hearing the song, Claire imagines returning home to her husband, Frank, where he greets her with a loving smile, wearing a Fair Isle vest cut in a classic style of the 1940s. It is knitted in the round from the bottom up, working steeks at the neck and arm openings, so that the stranded knitting can always be done with the right side of the work facing you.

SKILLS REQUIRED

Working in the round, working from charts, steeking, picking up stitches

MATERIALS

Trendsetter Yarns Merino 6 (100% extrafine merino wool; 136yds/124m per 1.75oz/50g ball)

Sample uses the following colors:

MC: color 779/Toffee; 5 (5, 6, 6, 7) balls

CC1: color 86277/Blue; 3 (3, 4, 4, 5) balls

CC2: color 9940/Butter; 2 (2, 3, 3, 3) balls

CC3: color 246/Watermelon; 1 ball

CC4: color 305/Charcoal; 1 ball

Substitution Notes: Look for a yarn with a fairly smooth texture and a significant amount of natural animal fiber, which will lend itself well to steeking. To re-create the colors in Frank's vest, you will need a light-to-medium warm brown as the main color, and, for the contrast colors: a pale blue, a pale yellow, a medium pinkish red, and a dark gray.

NEEDLES

US #3/3.25mm circular needle for the body: 32 inches/80cm (3 smaller sizes) or 40 to 47 inch/100 to 120cm circular needle (2 larger sizes)

US #4/3.5mm circular needle for the body: 32 inches/80cm (3 smaller sizes) or 40 to 47 inches/100 to 120cm circular needle for the body

US #3/3.25 16 inches/40cm circular needle for the armholes

Spare US #4/3.5mm circular, straight, or double-pointed needles for the three-needle bind-off

Or size needed to obtain gauge

NOTIONS

Stitch markers, including a distinctive one to mark the beginning of the round

Stitch holders

Safety pin

Crochet hook, or sewing machine and sewing thread, for reinforcing steeks

Yarn needle

GAUGE

22 sts/30 rounds = 4 inches/10cm square in stockinette stitch, using the larger needle

25 sts/27 rounds = 4 inches/10cm square in chart pattern after blocking, using the larger needle

SIZES

S (M, L, XL, 2XL)

FINISHED MEASUREMENTS

Garment should be worn with 3 to 4 inches/7.5 to 10cm ease. Choose a size 3 to 4 inches/7.5 to 10cm larger than your upper bust/chest measurement.

This garment is intended to fall at about 2 inches/ 5cm below the waistline.

A (chest circumference): 37.75 (42.25, 46.5, 51, 55) inches/96 (107.5, 118, 129.5, 139.5) cm

B (total height): 25.25 (27.25, 28.25, 30, 31) inches/64 (69, 72, 76, 78.5) cm

C (back width above armholes, including ribbing): 16.75 (17.75, 19, 19.25, 20.75) inches/42.5 (45, 48.5, 49, 52.5) cm

D (back neck, including ribbing): 6.75 (7, 7.25, 7.5, 7.75) inches/17 (18, 18.5, 19, 19.5) cm

E (neck depth, including ribbing): 7 (7.5, 7.5, 7.75, 8) inches/18 (19, 19, 19.5, 20.5) cm

F (armhole depth, including ribbing): 8.5

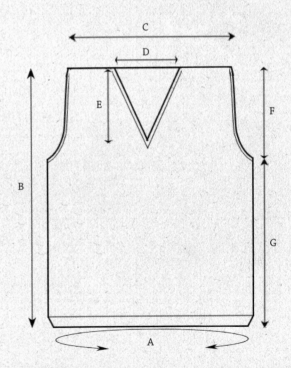

(9.25, 9.5, 10, 10.75) inches/21.5 (23.5, 24, 25.5, 27.5) cm

G (body length to underarm): 16.25 (17.25, 17.75, 19.25, 19.5) inches/41.5 (44, 45, 49, 49.5) cm

PATTERN NOTES

The vest is worked bottom up and in the round; steeks are used for the openings at the armholes, the front neck, and the back neck. There are side shaping decreases at the bottom of the armholes. Once the steeks have been cut open, ribbing is worked around the armholes and the neck opening.

MODIFICATIONS

The garment can be shortened by working fewer pattern rounds between the ribbing and the split for the armholes. The garment can be lengthened by working either longer ribbing, more pattern rounds between the ribbing and the split for the armholes, or both, depending on your personal preference.

COLORWORK PATTERN

The "DC" (dominant color) column indicates the color that should be held dominant as you work each round (see Tips on page 109).

INSTRUCTIONS

BODY

With MC and the smaller body needle, CO 212 (236, 262, 286, 310) sts using the long-tail cast-on. Pm for the beginning of the round and join in the round, being careful not to twist.

Round 1: (K1, p1) around.

FOR SIZE S

Inc round: *(K8, kfb) 5 times, k7, kfb; rep from * 3 more times. 236 sts.

COLORWORK PATTERN   KEY

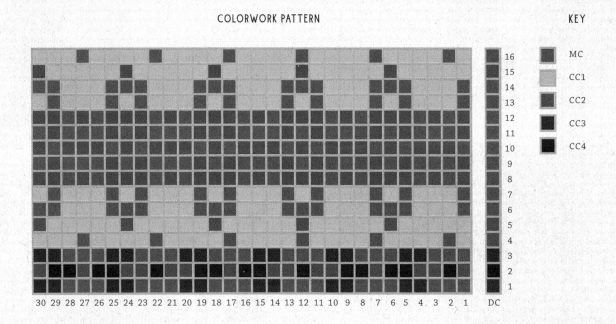

■	MC
■	CC1
■	CC2
■	CC3
■	CC4

SEASON
1

EPISODE
3

FOR SIZE 2XL

Inc round: *(K8, kfb) 7 times, k9, kfb, (k8, kfb) 8 times, k9, kfb; rep from * once more. 344 sts.

FOR ALL SIZES

Switch to the larger body needle. Join in additional colors as needed as you work the pattern rounds.

Round 1: *Begin with st 1 (1, 30, 29, 1) and work through 3 (4, 4, 5, 5) full repeats of the colorwork pattern chart (sts 1–30), work st 1 through st 28 (12, 24, 7, 22); pm, rep from * once more.

Cont patt as set, rep Rounds 1–16 of the colorwork pattern chart, until the body is 16.25 (17.25, 17.75, 19.25, 19.5) inches/41.5 (44, 45, 49, 49.5) cm from the cast-on edge.

ARMHOLE SHAPING

Round 1: Work in patt as set until 6 (8, 9, 12, 13) sts before the next marker, place the next 12 (16, 18, 24, 26) sts on a holder, removing the marker as you come to it, pm, CO 10 steek sts as follows: 1 st in the edge color, alternating colors for 8 sts, 1 st in the edge color; pm, work in patt as set until 6 (8, 9, 12, 13) sts rem, place the next 12 (16, 18, 24, 26) sts on a holder, removing the beginning of round marker as you come to it, pm, CO 10 steek sts as follows: 1 st in the edge color, alternating colors for 8 sts, 1 st in the edge color, pm for the beginning of rounds. 232 (252, 274, 290, 312) sts: 212 (232, 254, 270, 292) patt sts and 20 steek sts.

All the markers placed on this round serve to mark the beginning and end of the steek sts at the sides of the garment.

Round 2: Using the 2 colors indicated in the next row of the chart pattern, and slipping the markers as you come to them, *k2tog in patt, work patt as set to 2 sts before the next marker, ssk in patt, k1 in the edge color, k8 in alternating colors, k1 in the edge color; rep from * once more. 4 sts decreased.

FOR SIZE M

Inc round: *(K8, kfb, k7, kfb) 3 times, k7, kfb; rep from * 3 more times. 264 sts.

FOR SIZE L

Inc round: *K8, kfb, (k8, kfb, k9, kfb, k8, kfb) 4 times, k9, kfb; rep from * once more. 290 sts.

FOR SIZE XL

Inc round: *(K8, kfb) 15 times, k7, kfb; rep from * once more. 318 sts.

Rep the last round 4 (6, 8, 11, 12) more times. 212 (224, 238, 242, 260) sts: 192 (204, 218, 222, 240) patt sts and 20 steek sts.

Work 4 (4, 5, 3, 4) more rounds in patt as set without shaping.

NECK SHAPING

Round 1: Work 46 (49, 52, 53, 58) sts in patt as set, ssk in patt, place the next 0 (0, 1, 1, 0) st(s) on a safety pin, pm, CO 10 steek sts as follows: 1 st in the edge color, alternating colors for 8 sts, 1 st in the edge color; pm, k2tog in patt, work patt as set across the rem sts to the end of the round. 220 (232, 245, 249, 268) sts: 190 (202, 215, 219, 238) patt sts and 30 steek sts. Specifically, there are 47 (50, 53, 54, 59) left front sts, 10 front steek sts, 47 (50, 53, 54, 59) right front sts, 10 right steek sts, 96 (102, 109, 111, 120) back sts, and 10 left steek sts. The 2 new markers placed on this round mark the beginning and end of the front steek sts.

Round 2: Work patt as set.

Round 3: Work patt as set to 2 sts before the first marker, ssk in patt, work patt as set over 10 front steek sts, k2tog in patt, work pattern as set to the end of the round. 2 sts decreased.

Round 4: Rep Round 2.

Rep the last 2 rounds 21 (22, 22, 23, 24) more times, ending with an even round. 176 (186, 199, 201, 218) sts: 146 (156, 169, 171, 188) pattern sts and 30 steek sts. Specifically, there are 25 (27, 30, 30, 34) left front sts, 10 front steek sts, 25 (27, 30, 30, 34) right front sts, 10 right steek sts, 96 (102, 109, 111, 120) back sts, and 10 left steek sts.

BACK NECK SHAPING

Round 1: Work patt as set to 2 sts before the first marker, ssk in patt, work patt as set over 10 front steek sts, k2tog in patt, work patt as set over the rem right front patt sts and the 10 right steek sts, work patt as set over the next 23 (25, 28, 28, 32) patt sts, ssk in patt, place the next 46 (48,

- When picking up stitches along the edges of the armholes and the neck opening, the ratio will be approximately 2 sts for every 3 rounds.

- When picking up stitches along the edges of the armholes and the neck opening, use the edge sts of the steeks.

- It is recommended that you anchor strands vertically up the work when colors won't be used for more than four rounds. For example, you will want to anchor CC3 a few times after working Round 3 of the chart, as it will be 14 rounds before it is used again. Alternatively, you can cut and rejoin these colors, but this will involve weaving in a lot of ends when finishing.

- In stranded knitting, the concept of color dominance is important. When working with two colors, one color will stand out more clearly, depending on how the two colors are floated at the wrong side of the work. On each row, one color's floats will be positioned above the other color's floats: the top floats will be the background color, and the bottom floats will be the color that dominates at the right side of the work. To assist you in keeping consistency throughout the stranded pattern, the recommended dominant color is provided for each row of the chart, to the immediate right of the row number, marked as DC.

- Once you start steeking, "edge color" in the instructions means either:

  If MC is being used in a round: MC.

  If MC is not being used in a round: CC2.

49, 51, 52) sts on a holder, pm, CO 10 steek sts in your preferred method as follows: 1 st in the edge color, alternating colors for 8 sts, 1 st in the edge color; pm, k2tog in patt, work patt as set to the end of the round. 136 (144, 156, 156, 172) sts: 96 (104, 116, 116, 132) patt sts and 40 steek sts. Specifically, there are 24 (26, 29, 29, 33) left front sts, 10 front steek sts, 24 (26, 29, 29, 33) right front sts, 10 right steek sts, 24 (26, 29, 29, 33) right back sts, 10 back steek sts, 24 (26, 29, 29, 33) left back sts, and 10 left steek sts. The 2 new markers placed on this round mark the beginning and the end of the back steek sts.

Round 2: Work even in patt as set.

Round 3: Work patt as set to 2 sts before the first neck steek marker, ssk in patt, work patt as set over the 10 front steek sts, k2tog in patt, work patt as set to 2 sts before the first back steek marker, ssk in patt, work patt as set over 10 back steek sts, k2tog in patt, work patt as set across the rem sts. 4 sts decreased.

Round 4: Rep Round 2.

Rep the last 2 rounds once more. 128 (136, 148, 148, 164) sts: 22 (24, 27, 27, 31) left front sts, 10 front steek sts, 22 (24, 27, 27, 31) right front sts, 10 right steek sts, 22 (24, 27, 27, 31) right back sts, 10 back steek sts, 22 (24, 27, 27, 31) left back sts, and 10 left steek sts.

Next round: Removing markers as you come to them, *work patt as set over the next 22 (24, 27, 27, 31) sts, BO 10 steek sts in patt; rep from * 3 more times. 88 (96, 108, 108, 124) sts.

Break all yarns.

FINISHING

With WS facing, and making sure not to twist your work, use MC and the three-needle BO to join the 22 (24, 27, 27, 31) left front sts to the 22 (24, 27, 27, 31) left back sts. Rep with the 22 (24, 27, 27, 31) right front sts to the 22 (24, 27, 27, 31) right back sts.

STEEKING

With MC (if crocheting) or sewing thread (if sewing), reinforce all steeks and then cut them all open up the center between the fifth and sixth steek sts.

ARMHOLE RIBBING

Pickup round: Using MC, and with RS facing, place the 12 (16, 18, 24, 26) sts at the bottom of the armhole onto the short smaller circular needle and knit them; pick up 2 sts in the corner between the bottom and the side of the armhole and knit them together, pick up and knit 42 (45, 47, 49, 52) sts up the side of the armhole, pick up and knit 42 (45, 47, 49, 52) sts down the other side of the armhole, pick up 2 sts in the corner between the side and the bottom of the armhole and knit them together, pm for the beginning of the round. 98 (108, 114, 124, 132) sts.

Ribbing round 1: (K1, p1) around.

Rep the last round until the ribbing measures 0.75 inches/2cm. BO in patt.

NECK RIBBING

Pickup round: Using MC, and with RS facing, place the 46 (48, 49, 51, 52) back neck sts onto the short smaller circular needle and knit them, pick up 2 sts in the corner between the bottom and the edge of the back and knit them together, pick up and knit 5 sts up the left back neck edge, pick up 2 sts between the back and front and knit them together, pick up and knit 36 (37, 37, 38, 40) sts down the left front neck edge, pick up 2 sts in the corner between the sts just worked and the center front point and knit them together, pm, k0 (0, 1, 1, 0) st(s) from the safety pin, pick up 2 sts in the corner between the sts just worked and the right front edge and knit them together, pick up and knit 36 (37, 37, 38, 40) sts up the right front neck edge, pick up 2 sts in the corner between the front and back and knit them together, pick up and knit 5 sts down the right back neck edge, pick up 2 sts in the corner between the edge and bottom of the back and knit them together, pm for the beginning of the round. 134 (138, 140, 144, 148) sts. The marker you placed near the center front is to help alert you when decreases need to be made on subsequent rounds.

Round 1: P1 (0, 1, 0, 1), (k1, p1) to 1 st before center marker, sl 1, rm, transfer the st from the left-hand needle back to the right-hand needle, pm, CDD, (p1, k1) 21 (22, 22, 22, 23) times, p0 (1, 0, 1, 0). 132 (136, 138, 142, 146) sts.

Round 2: Work in ribbing patt as set to 1 st before the center marker, sl 1, rm, transfer the st from left-hand needle back to the right-hand needle, pm, CDD, work in ribbing patt as set to the end. 2 sts decreased.

Rep the last round until the ribbing measures 0.75 inches/2cm. Your stitch count will vary depending on how many rounds you worked to achieve this length; the exact number is not important as long as you decrease 2 sts at the center front on each round and the ribbing measures 0.75 inches/2cm.

BO in patt, removing all markers as you come to them.

Soak, using a wool wash if desired. Remove from the water, press most of the moisture out, and lay it flat to dry, gently shaping the garment as required. Leave to dry.

Trim steeks to 2-st widths and secure them at the inside of the work. Weave in all remaining ends at the inside of the work.

SEASON
1

EPISODE
7

THE IMPORTANCE
of Wool

As knitters, we all know and understand the value of wool, and members of the *Outlander* costume department learned early in the production: if it was cold inside the stone castle, shooting outside was going to be even worse. After all, actors need to be kept warm and dry while waiting sometimes long periods between takes. This is a show with plenty of outdoor action, often with many characters, and the costume team was worried about them.

The costume department members understood why wool is so prevalent in vintage and traditional Scottish garb: not only does it keep you warm, but it also keeps you dry. After one particularly epic shoot in a downpour, the actors were pleasantly surprised to find themselves just as comfortable in their period-appropriate woolies as the shooting crew was in their modern weatherproof gear.

I FOUND HIM
Lace Cardigan

Designed by Holli Yeoh

Claire's 1960s fashion sense is classic and understated. She dresses for function but, as a professional and a doctor, she also presents herself with well-tailored clothes and indulges in luxe fabrics and fibers. While in Scotland researching Jamie's fate, Claire spent a lot of time in the Reverend's study. This cardigan is inspired by the crocheted cardigan she wore while reading Ardsmuir Prison's annual rolls from the 1750s and discovered that Jamie survived Culloden.

SKILLS REQUIRED

Lace, short rows, picking up stitches, seaming

MATERIALS

Cardiff Cashmere Yarn Classic (100% cashmere; 122yds/112m per 0.88oz/25g skein); 10 (11, 12, 13, 14, 15, 16, 18, 19, 20) skeins

Sample uses color 652/Mafalda (Plum).

Substitution Notes: Cardiff Cashmere is a lofty DK yarn that is airy, luxurious, and soft. A sturdier yarn of the same weight would also work for this design; it would just create a more structured cardigan. The key is to obtain gauge while creating a fabric that has some drape.

NEEDLES

US #3/3.25mm needles for working flat

US #4/3.5mm needles for working flat

US #5/3.75mm needles for working flat

US #6/4mm needles for working flat

US #7/4.5mm needles for working flat

Or size needed to obtain gauge

NOTIONS

Cable needle

Stitch markers

Yarn needle

9 (9, 9, 9, 9, 9, 10, 10, 10, 10) 9/16-inch/14mm buttons

Sewing needle and matching thread

56 (57, 58, 59, 59, 60, 61, 61, 62, 63) inches/142 (145, 147.5, 150, 150, 152.5, 155, 155, 157.5, 160) cm 5/8-inch/16mm grosgrain ribbon (optional)

9 (9, 9, 9, 9, 9, 10, 10, 10, 10) 0.25-inch/6mm snaps (optional)

GAUGE

21 sts/31 rows = 4 inches/10cm square in stockinette stitch, using US #6/4mm needles

19 sts/32 rows = 4 inches/10cm square in pattern stitch, using US #6/4mm needles

SIZES

XS (S, M, L, XL, 2XL, 3XL, 4XL, 5XL, 6XL)

FINISHED MEASUREMENTS

This garment should be worn with 2 to 3 inches/5 to 7.5cm ease. Choose a size 2 to 3 inches/5 to 7.5cm larger than your upper bust/chest measurement.

A (back width): 17.5 (18.75, 20, 22, 23.75, 26, 28, 30, 31.75, 34) inches/44.5 (47.5, 51, 56, 60.5, 66, 71, 76, 80.5, 86.5) cm

B (back width above armholes): 14 (14.5, 15, 15.25, 15.75, 16.75, 17, 18, 18.75, 20) inches/35.5 (37, 38, 38.5, 40, 42.5, 43, 45.5, 47.5, 51) cm

C (back neck width): 7.25 (7.75, 7.75, 8.25, 8.25, 8.25, 8.25, 8.75, 8.75) inches/18.5 (19.5, 19.5, 21, 21, 21, 21, 21, 22, 22) cm

D (shoulder width): 3.25 (3.25, 3.5, 3.5, 3.75, 4.25, 4.5, 4.75, 5, 5.75) inches/8 (8, 9, 9, 9.5, 11, 11.5, 12, 12.5, 14.5) cm

E (length to underarm): 14 (14.5, 14.75, 15.25, 15.25, 15, 15.25, 15.25, 15.75, 16) inches/35.5 (37, 37.5, 38.5, 38.5, 38, 38.5, 39.5, 40, 40.5) cm

F (back armhole depth): 4.75 (5, 5, 5.25, 5.5, 5.75, 6, 6.25, 6.5, 6.75) inches/12 (12.5, 12.5, 13.5, 14, 14.5, 15, 16, 16.5, 17) cm

G (shoulder depth): 3 (3, 3.25, 3.25, 3.25, 3.5, 3.5, 3.5, 3.5, 3.5) inches/7.5 (7.5, 8.5, 8.5, 8.5, 9, 9, 9, 9, 9) cm

H (total length): 21.75 (22.5, 23, 23.75, 24, 24.25, 24.75, 25.25, 25.75, 26.25) inches/55 (57, 58.5, 60.5, 61, 61.5, 63, 64, 65.5, 66.5) cm

I (front width): 8.75 (9.25, 10, 11, 11.75, 12.75, 14, 15, 15.75, 16.75) inches/22 (23.5, 25.5, 28, 30, 32.5, 35.5, 38, 40, 42.5) cm

J (front armhole depth): 8.75 (9, 9, 9.25, 9.5, 9.75, 10, 10.25, 10.5, 10.75) inches/22 (23, 23, 23.5, 24, 25, 25.5, 26, 26.5, 27.5) cm

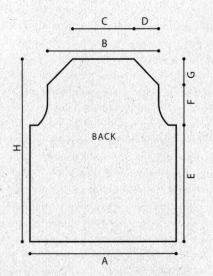

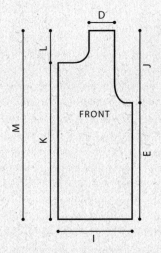

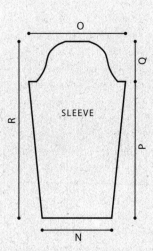

K (front edge length): 19 (19.5, 19.75, 20.5, 20.5, 20.75, 21.25, 21.25, 22, 22.5) inches/48.5 (49.5, 50, 52, 52, 52.5, 54, 54, 56, 57) cm

L (front neck depth): 3.75 (4, 4, 4, 4.25, 4, 4, 4.25, 4.25, 4.25) inches/9.5 (10, 10, 10, 11, 10, 10, 11, 11, 11) cm

M (total front length): 22.75 (23.5, 23.75, 24.5, 24.75, 24.75, 25.25, 25.75, 26.25, 26.75) inches/58 (59.5, 60.5, 62, 63, 63, 64, 65.5, 66.5, 68) cm

N (wrist circumference): 8.75 (8.75, 8.75, 8.75, 9, 9, 9, 9, 9, 9) inches/22 (22, 22, 22, 23, 23, 23, 23, 23, 23) cm

O (upper arm circumference): 12 (12.5, 13.25, 14, 15.25, 16.75, 18, 19.5, 20.75, 22.5) inches/30.5 (32, 33.5, 35.5, 38.5, 42.5, 45.5, 49.5, 52.5, 57) cm

P (sleeve length from wrist to underarm): 16.5 (17, 17, 17.5, 17.5, 18, 18, 18.5, 18.5, 18.5) inches/42 (43, 43, 44.5, 44.5, 45.5, 45.5, 47, 47, 47) cm

Q (sleeve cap height): 4.75 (5, 5, 5.5, 5.5, 5.75, 6, 6, 6.25, 6.25) inches/12 (12.5, 12.5, 14, 14, 14.5, 15, 15, 16, 16) cm

R (total sleeve length): 21.25 (22, 22, 23, 23, 23.75, 24, 24.5, 24.75, 24.75) inches/54 (56, 56, 58.5, 58.5, 60.5, 61, 62, 63, 63) cm

PATTERN NOTES

This cardigan is worked flat, in pieces from the bottom up. The Diamond Eyelet pattern is worked all over and carefully calculated to match at the side seams. Back shoulder shaping is fully fashioned with double decreases, and the front shoulders are worked straight with deeper armholes than the back. Sleeves are bracelet length. Front bands, which are picked up and worked out, are reinforced with grosgrain ribbon. If you're substituting with a sturdier yarn, this may not be required. The collar is picked up around the neckline with a small needle and worked with short rows across the back neck, then worked with progressively larger needles. This helps the collar fold over and not stand up.

MODIFICATIONS

To change the length of the cardigan, work fewer or more rows before the underarm bind-off on both fronts and back. To change the length of the sleeves, add or subtract length after the shaping rows are completed and before making the sleeve cap.

For example: If you're working a 4XL sweater size with 5XL sleeves, the total sleeve width difference is 6 sts ("A"). Work the first 3 dec rows ("B") with an extra decrease at each end of the row. The first row should have a double dec, so work a triple dec. The next two dec rows should be single decs, so work them as double decs. Work the remaining decs as instructed for your original size.

If your row gauge is wildly different than the pattern gauge, the sleeve cap won't fit the armhole. Measure your row gauge. Multiply the sleeve cap height (from the schematic) by the pattern row gauge ("A"). Multiply the sleeve cap height by your row gauge ("B"). Subtract B from A (A − B = C) to get the number of rows you need to add or subtract from your sleeve cap; round this to an even number. If you need to subtract rows, take them from the section where you work the decrease row every fourth row. If you need to add rows, add them in the section where the decrease rows are worked every second row. The key is to keep the sleeve cap the same depth as the original pattern.

DIAMOND EYELET PATTERN
(multiple of 12 plus 3): for swatching ONLY

Work from the chart or the written instructions, whichever you prefer.

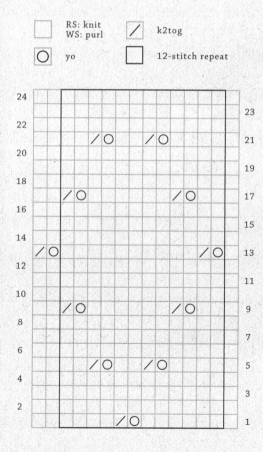

KEY

| | RS: knit WS: purl | / | k2tog |
| O | yo | | 12-stitch repeat |

Row 1 (RS): K1, *k6, yo, k2tog, k4; rep from * to the last 2 sts, k2.

Row 2 (and all WS rows): Purl.

Row 3: Knit.

Row 5: K1, *k4, (yo, k2tog, k2) twice; rep from * to the last 2 sts, k2.

Row 7: Knit.

Row 9: K1, *k2, yo, k2tog, k6, yo, k2tog; rep from * to the last 2 sts, k2.

Row 11: Knit.

Row 13: K1, *yo, k2tog, k10; rep from * to the last 2 sts, yo, k2tog.

Row 15: Knit.

Row 17: Rep Row 9.

Row 19: Knit.

Row 21: Rep Row 5.

Row 23: Knit.

Row 24: Purl.

Rows 1–24 form the Diamond Eyelet pattern.

SPECIAL STITCHES

2decB (double cabled decrease back): Transfer 2 sts onto the cable needle and hold at back, (knit the first st on the left-hand needle tog with the first st on the cable needle) 2 times. 2 sts decreased.

2decF (double cabled decrease front): Transfer 2 sts onto the cable needle and hold at front, (knit the first st on cable needle tog with the first st on the left-hand needle) 2 times. 2 sts decreased.

GERMAN SHORT ROWS

Work to the turning point; turn. With yarn in front, slip the first stitch purlwise. Bring the yarn over the back of the right needle, pulling firmly to create a double stitch on the right needle. If the next stitch is a knit stitch, leave the yarn at the back; if the next stitch is a purl stitch, bring the yarn to the front between the needles. When it's time to work into the double stitch, knit both strands together.

RUSSIAN BIND-OFF

K1, *k1, transfer both sts back to the left needle, k2tog tbl; rep from * until all required sts have been worked.

~~~~~~~~~~~~~~~~~~~~~~~~~~~~~~

INSTRUCTIONS

BACK

With US #4/3.5mm needles, CO 86 (92, 101, 110, 119, 131, 140, 149, 161, 170) sts.

Row 1 (RS): Knit.

Row 2 (WS): *P2, k1; rep from * to the last 2 sts, p2.

Work 12 (12, 12, 12, 12, 14, 14, 14, 14, 14) rows more in ribbing as set, ending with a WS row.

Change to US #6/4mm needles.

Dec row (RS): K11 (14, 5, 11, 5, 11, 5, 14, 11, 11), k2tog, *k28 (28, 16, 19, 19, 13, 19, 22, 13, 16), k2tog; rep from * 1 (1, 4, 3, 4, 6, 5, 4, 8, 7) time(s) more, knit rem 13 (16, 4, 13, 7, 13, 7, 13, 13, 13) sts. 83 (89, 95, 105, 113, 123, 133, 143, 151, 161) sts.

Purl 1 WS row.

BEGIN DIAMOND EYELET PATTERN

Note: The last lace rep of every RS row will be incomplete for most sizes.

Row 1 (RS): K11 (8, 11, 10, 8, 7, 12, 11, 9, 8), *yo, k2tog, k10; rep from * ending with k0 (9, 0, 11, 9, 8, 1, 0, 10, 9).

Row 2 (and all WS rows): Purl.

Row 3: Knit.

Row 5: K1 (6, 1, 8, 6, 5, 2, 1, 7, 6), [yo, k2tog, k6] 1 (0, 1, 0, 0, 0, 1, 1, 0, 0) time(s), *yo, k2tog, k2, yo, k2tog, k6; rep from * ending with k0 (5, 0, 7, 5, 4, 1, 0, 6, 5).

Row 7: Knit.

Row 9: K3 (4, 3, 2, 4, 3, 4, 3, 1, 4), [yo, k2tog, k2] 1 (0, 1, 1, 0, 0, 1, 1, 1, 0) time(s), *yo, k2tog, k6, yo, k2tog, k2; rep from * ending with k2 (3, 2, 1, 3, 2, 3, 2, 0, 3).

Row 11: Knit.

Row 13: K5 (2, 5, 4, 2, 1, 6, 5, 3, 2), *yo, k2tog, k10; rep from * ending with k4 (1, 4, 3, 1, 0, 5, 4, 2, 1).

Row 15: Knit.

Row 17: Rep Row 9.

Row 19: Knit.

Row 21: Rep Row 5.

Row 23: Knit.

Rows 1–24 form the Diamond Eyelet pattern.

Work even in the Diamond Eyelet pattern until the piece measures 14 (14.5, 14.75, 15.25, 15.25, 15, 15.25, 15.5, 15.75, 16) inches/35.5 (37, 37.5, 38.5, 38.5, 38, 38.5, 39.5, 40, 40.5) cm from beg, ending with a WS row.

ARMHOLE SHAPING

BO 4 (5, 6, 8, 10, 9, 10, 10, 12, 12) sts at beg of the next 2 rows, maintaining patt. 75 (79, 83, 89, 93, 105, 113, 123, 127, 137) sts rem.

FOR SIZES 2XL, 3XL, 4XL, 5XL, 6XL ONLY

Double dec row (RS): K2, 2decB, work in patt to last 5 sts, 2decF, k2. 4 sts decreased.

Work 1 WS row.

Working in patt, rep double dec row every RS row – (–, –, –, –, 0, 0, 1, 1, 2) time(s) more. – (–, –, –, –, 101, 109, 115, 119, 125) sts rem.

FOR ALL SIZES

Dec row (RS): K2, k2tog, work in patt to the last 4 sts, ssk, k2. 2 sts decreased.

Work 1 WS row.

Working in patt, rep the dec row every RS row 3 (4, 5, 7, 8, 10, 13, 14, 14, 14) times more. 67 (69, 71, 73, 75, 79, 81, 85, 89, 95) sts rem.

Work even in patt until the armhole measures 4.75 (5, 5, 5.25, 5.5, 5.75, 6, 6.25, 6.5, 6.75) inches/12 (12.5, 12.5, 13.5, 14, 14.5, 15, 16, 16.5, 17) cm from underarm BO, ending with a WS row.

SHOULDER SHAPING

Double dec row (RS): K2, 2decB, work in patt to the last 6 sts, 2decF, k2. 4 sts decreased.

Work 1 WS row.

Working in patt, rep the double dec row every RS row 3 (3, 3, 3, 4, 5, 6, 8, 9, 12) times more, ending with a WS row. 51 (53, 55, 57, 55, 55, 53, 49, 49, 43) sts rem.

Single dec row (RS): K2, k2tog, work in patt to the last 4 sts, ssk, k2. 2 sts decreased.

Work 1 WS row.

Working in patt, rep the single dec row every RS row 7 (7, 8, 8, 7, 7, 6, 4, 3, 0) time(s) more, ending with a WS row. 35 (37, 37, 39, 39, 39, 39, 39, 41, 41) sts rem.

BO all sts.

LEFT FRONT

With US #4/3.5mm needles, CO 42 (45, 48, 54, 57, 63, 66, 72, 78, 81) sts.

Row 1 (RS): Knit.

Row 2 (WS): P3, *k1, p2; rep from * to the end of the row.

Work 12 (12, 12, 12, 12, 14, 14, 14, 14, 14) rows more in ribbing as set.

Change to US #6/4mm needles.

FOR SIZES XS, S, XL, 4XL, 6XL ONLY

Dec row (RS): K5, k2tog, knit to the end of the row. 41 (44, –, –, 56, –, –, 71, –, 80) sts.

Purl 1 WS row.

FOR SIZES L, 2XL, 5XL ONLY

Dec row (RS): K– (–, –, 14, –, 14, –, –, 11, –), k2tog, *k– (–, –, 25, –, 31, –, –, 25, –), k2tog; rep from * – (–, –, 0, –, 0, –, –, 1, –) time(s) more, knit rem – (–, –, 11, –, 14, –, –, 11, –) sts. – (–, –, 52, –, 61, –, –, 75, –) sts rem.

Purl 1 WS row.

FOR ALL SIZES: BEGIN THE DIAMOND EYELET PATTERN

Note: The last lace rep of every RS row will be incomplete for most sizes.

Row 1: K2 (5, 2, 3, 5, 6, 1, 2, 4, 5), *yo, k2tog, k10; rep from *, ending with k1 (1, 8, 11, 1, 5, 3, 7, 9, 1).

Row 2 (and all WS rows): Purl.

Row 3: Knit.

Row 5: K4 (3, 4, 1, 3, 4, 3, 4, 2, 3), [yo, k2tog, k6] 1 (0, 1, 0, 0, 0, 1, 1, 0, 0) time(s), *yo, k2tog, k2, yo, k2tog, k6; rep from *, ending with k3 (3, 6, 1, 3, 3, 1, 5, 7, 3).

Row 7: Knit.

Row 9: K6 (1, 6, 7, 1, 2, 5, 6, 8, 1), [yo, k2tog, k2] 1 (0, 1, 1, 0, 0, 1, 1, 1, 0) time(s), *yo, k2tog, k6, yo, k2tog, k2; rep from *, ending with k5 (5, 4, 3, 5, 1, 7, 3, 1, 5).

Row 11: Knit.

Row 13: K8 (11, 8, 9, 11, 12, 7, 8, 10, 11), *yo, k2tog, k10; rep from *, ending with k7 (7, 2, 5, 7, 11, 9, 1, 3, 7).

Row 15: Knit.

Row 17: Rep Row 9.

Row 19: Knit.

Row 21: Rep Row 5.

Row 23: Knit.

Rows 1–24 form the Diamond Eyelet pattern.

Work even in patt until the piece measures 14 (14.5, 14.75, 15.25, 15.25, 15, 15.25, 15.5, 15.75, 16) inches/35.5 (37, 37.5, 38.5, 38.5, 38, 38.5, 39.5, 40, 40.5) cm from beg, ending with a WS row.

ARMHOLE SHAPING

BO 4 (5, 6, 8, 10, 9, 10, 10, 12, 12) sts at the beg of the next row, maintaining patt. 37 (39, 42, 44, 46, 52, 56, 61, 63, 68) sts rem.

Work 1 WS row.

FOR SIZES 2XL, 3XL, 4XL, 5XL, 6XL ONLY

Double dec row (RS): K2, 2decB, work in patt to the end of the row. 2 sts decreased.

Work 1 WS row.

Working in patt, rep the double dec row every RS row – (–, –, –, –, 0, 0, 1, 1, 2) time(s) more. – (–, –, –, –, 50, 54, 57, 59, 62) sts rem.

FOR ALL SIZES

Dec row (RS): K2, k2tog, work in patt to the end of the row. 1 st decreased.

Work 1 WS row.

Working in patt, rep the dec row every RS row 3 (4, 5, 7, 8, 10, 13, 14, 14, 14) times more. 33 (34, 36, 36, 37, 39, 40, 42, 44, 47) sts rem.

Work even in patt until armhole measures 5 (5, 5, 5.25, 5.25, 5.75, 6, 6, 6.25, 6.5) inches/12.5 (12.5, 12.5, 13.5, 13.5, 14.5, 15, 15, 16, 16.5) cm from the underarm BO, ending with a RS row.

NECK SHAPING

BO 8 (9, 10, 9, 9, 9, 9, 9, 10, 10) sts purlwise at the beg of the next row. 25 (25, 26, 27, 28, 30, 31, 33, 34, 37) sts rem.

Row 1 (and all RS rows): Work in patt to the last st, sl 1.

Row 2 (WS): Sl 2, pass first st over second st, BO 2 sts purlwise, purl to the end of the row. 22 (22, 23, 24, 25, 27, 28, 30, 31, 34) sts rem.

Row 4: Sl 2, pass first st over second st, BO 1 st purlwise, purl to the end of the row. 20 (20, 21, 22, 23, 25, 26, 28, 29, 32) sts rem.

Row 6: Rep Row 4. 18 (18, 19, 20, 21, 23, 24, 26, 27, 30) sts rem.

Row 8: Sl 2, pass first st over second st, purl to the end of the row. 1 st decreased.

Working in patt, rep Row 8 every WS row 1 (1, 1, 2, 2, 2, 2, 2, 2, 2) time(s) more. 16 (16, 17, 17, 18, 20, 21, 23, 24, 27) sts rem.

Work even in patt until the armhole measures 8.75 (9, 9, 9.25, 9.5, 9.75, 10, 10.25, 10.5, 10.75) inches/22 (23, 23, 23.5, 24, 25, 25.5, 26, 26.5, 27.5) cm from the underarm BO, ending with a WS row.

BO loosely with a needle 2 to 4 sizes larger.

RIGHT FRONT

With US #4/3.5mm needles, CO 42 (45, 48, 54, 57, 63, 66, 72, 78, 81) sts.

Row 1 (RS): Knit.

Row 2 (WS): *P2, k1; rep from * to the last 3 sts, p3.

Work 12 (12, 12, 12, 12, 14, 14, 14, 14, 14) rows more in ribbing as set.

Change to US #6/4mm needles.

FOR SIZES XS, S, XL, 4XL, 6XL ONLY

Dec row (RS): K3, k2tog, knit to the end of the row. 41 (44, –, –, 56, –, –, 71, –, 80) sts.

Purl 1 WS row.

FOR SIZES L, 2XL, 5XL ONLY

Dec row (RS): K– (–, –, 15, –, 15, –, –, 12, –), k2tog, *k– (–, –, 25, –, 31, –, –, 25, –), k2tog; rep from * – (–, –, 0, –, 0, –, –, 1, –) time(s) more, knit rem – (–, –, 10, –, 13, –, –, 10, –) sts. – (–, –, 52, –, 61, –, –, 75, –) sts rem.

Purl 1 WS row.

FOR ALL SIZES: BEGIN THE DIAMOND EYELET PATTERN

Note: The last lace rep of every RS row will be incomplete for most sizes.

Row 1 (RS): K2 (2, 9, 12, 2, 6, 4, 8, 10, 2), *yo, k2tog, k10; rep from *, ending with k1 (4, 1, 2, 4, 5, 0, 1, 3, 4).

Row 2 (and all WS rows): Purl.

Row 3: Knit.

Row 5: K4 (4, 7, 2, 4, 4, 2, 6, 8, 4), [yo, k2tog, k6] 1 (1, 0, 1, 1, 0, 0, 0, 1, 1) time(s), *yo, k2tog, k2, yo, k2tog, k6; rep from *, ending with k3 (2, 3, 0, 2, 3, 2, 3, 5, 2).

Row 7: Knit.

Row 9: K6 (6, 5, 4, 6, 2, 8, 4, 2, 6), [yo, k2tog, k2] 1 (1, 0, 1, 1, 1, 1, 0, 1, 1) time(s), *yo, k2tog, k6, yo, k2tog, k2; rep from *, ending with k5 (0, 5, 6, 0, 5, 4, 5, 7, 0).

Row 11: Knit.

Row 13: K8 (8, 3, 6, 8, 12, 10, 2, 4, 8), *yo, k2tog, k10; rep from *, ending with k7 (10, 7, 8, 10, 11, 6, 7, 9, 10).

Row 15: Knit.

Row 17: Rep Row 9.

Row 19: Knit.

Row 21: Rep Row 5.

Row 23: Knit.

Rows 1–24 form the Diamond Eyelet pattern.

Work even in patt until the piece measures 14 (14.5, 14.75, 15.25, 15.25, 15, 15.25, 15.5, 15.75, 16) inches/35.5 (37, 37.5, 38.5, 38.5, 38, 38.5, 39.5, 40, 40.5) cm from the beg, ending with a RS row.

ARMHOLE SHAPING

BO 4 (5, 6, 8, 10, 9, 10, 10, 12, 12) sts purlwise at the beg of the next row. 37 (39, 42, 44, 46, 52, 56, 61, 63, 68) sts rem.

FOR SIZES 2XL, 3XL, 4XL, 5XL, 6XL ONLY

Double dec row (RS): Work in patt to the last 5 sts, 2decF, k2. 2 sts decreased.

Work 1 WS row.

Working in patt, rep the double dec row every RS row – (–, –, –, –, 0, 0, 1, 1, 2) time(s) more. – (–, –, –, –, 50, 54, 57, 59, 62) sts rem.

FOR ALL SIZES

Dec row (RS): Work in patt to the last 4 sts, ssk, k2. 1 st decreased.

Work 1 WS row.

Working in patt, rep the dec row every RS row 3

(4, 5, 7, 8, 10, 13, 14, 14, 14) times more. 33 (34, 36, 36, 37, 39, 40, 42, 44, 47) sts rem.

Work even in patt until the armhole measures 5 (5, 5, 5.25, 5.25, 5.75, 6, 6, 6.25, 6.5) inches/12.5 (12.5, 12.5, 13.5, 13.5, 14.5, 15, 15, 16, 16.5) cm from the underarm BO, ending with a WS row.

NECK SHAPING

BO 8 (9, 10, 9, 9, 9, 9, 9, 10, 10) sts at the beg of the next row. 25 (25, 26, 27, 28, 30, 31, 33, 34, 37) sts rem.

Row 1 (and all WS rows): Purl to the last st, sl 1.

Row 2 (RS): Sl 2, pass first st over second st, BO 2 sts, work in patt to the end of the row. 22 (22, 23, 24, 25, 27, 28, 30, 31, 34) sts rem.

Row 4: Sl 2, pass first st over second st, BO 1 st, work in patt to the end of the row. 20 (20, 21, 22, 23, 25, 26, 28, 29, 32) sts rem.

Row 6: Rep Row 4. 18 (18, 19, 20, 21, 23, 24, 26, 27, 30) sts rem.

Row 8: Sl 2, pass first st over second st, work in patt to the end of the row. 1 st decreased.

Working in patt, rep Row 8 every RS row 1 (1, 1, 2, 2, 2, 2, 2, 2, 2) time(s) more. 16 (16, 17, 17, 18, 20, 21, 23, 24, 27) sts rem.

Work even in patt until the armhole measures 8.75 (9, 9, 9.25, 9.5, 9.75, 10, 10.25, 10.5, 10.75) inches/22 (23, 23, 23.5, 24, 25, 25.5, 26, 26.5, 27.5) cm from the underarm BO, ending with a WS row.

BO loosely with a needle 2 to 4 sizes larger.

SLEEVE

With US #4/3.5mm needles, CO 41 (41, 41, 41, 44, 44, 47, 47, 47, 47) sts.

Row 1 (RS): Knit.

Row 2 (WS): *P2, k1; rep from * to last 2 sts, p2.

Work 6 rows more in ribbing as set.

Change to US #6/4mm needles.

SEASON
3
EPISODE
4

127

FOR SIZES XS, S, M, L ONLY

Knit 1 RS row.

FOR SIZES XL, 2XL ONLY

Dec row (RS): K5, k2tog, knit to the end of the row. 43 sts rem.

FOR SIZES 3XL, 4XL, 5XL, 6XL ONLY

Dec row (RS): K5, k2tog, *k10, k2tog; rep from * twice more, knit rem 4 sts. 43 sts rem.

FOR ALL SIZES

Purl 1 WS row.

BEGIN THE DIAMOND EYELET PATTERN

Row 1 (RS): K8 (8, 8, 8, 9, 9, 9, 9, 9, 9), *yo, k2tog, k10; rep from *, ending with k7 (7, 7, 7, 8, 8, 8, 8, 8, 8).

Row 2 (and all WS rows through Row 24): Purl.

Row 3: Knit.

Row 5: K6 (6, 6, 6, 7, 7, 7, 7, 7, 7), *yo, k2tog, k2, yo, k2tog, k6; rep from *, ending with k5 (5, 5, 5, 6, 6, 6, 6, 6, 6).

Row 7: Knit.

Row 9: K4 (4, 4, 4, 5, 5, 5, 5, 5, 5), *yo, k2tog, k6, yo, k2tog, k2; rep from *, ending with k3 (3, 3, 3, 4, 4, 4, 4, 4, 4).

Row 11: Knit.

Row 13: K2 (2, 2, 2, 3, 3, 3, 3, 3, 3), *yo, k2tog, k10; rep from *, ending with k1 (1, 1, 1, 2, 2, 2, 2, 2, 2).

Row 15: Knit.

Row 17: Rep Row 9.

Row 19: Knit.

Row 21: Rep Row 5.

Row 23: Knit.

Rows 1–24 form the Diamond Eyelet pattern.

SLEEVE SHAPING

While working new sts into the patt, it's recommended that there are at least 2 sts between any yarnover and the outer edge. Continue the Diamond Eyelet pattern while working the shaping as follows:

Inc row (RS): K2, RLI, knit to the last 2 sts, LLI, k2. 2 sts increased.

Working in patt, rep the inc row every 10 (8, 6, 6, 4, 4, 4, 2, 2, 2) rows 5 (1, 1, 7, 1, 8, 17, 3, 9, 17) time(s) more. 53 (45, 45, 57, 47, 61, 79, 51, 63, 79) sts.

Rep the inc row every 12 (10, 8, 8, 6, 6, 6, 4, 4, 4) rows 2 (7, 9, 5, 13, 9, 3, 21, 18, 14) time(s). 57 (59, 63, 67, 73, 79, 85, 93, 99, 107) sts.

Work even until the sleeve measures 16.5 (17, 17, 17.5, 17.5, 18, 18, 18.5, 18.5, 18.5) inches/42 (43, 43, 44.5, 44.5, 45.5, 45.5, 47, 47, 47) cm from the beg, ending with a WS row.

SLEEVE CAP SHAPING

Working in patt, BO 4 (5, 6, 8, 10, 9, 10, 10, 12, 12) sts at the beg of the next 2 rows. 49 (49, 51, 51, 53, 61, 65, 73, 75, 83) sts.

FOR SIZES 4XL, 5XL, 6XL ONLY

Double dec row (RS): K2, 2decB, Work in patt to the last 5 sts, 2decF, k2. 4 sts decreased.

Work 1 WS row.

Rep the double dec row every RS row – (–, –, –, –, –, –, 0, 0, 4) times more, ending with a WS row. – (–, –, –, –, –, –, 69, 71, 63) sts.

FOR ALL SIZES

Single dec row (RS): K2, k2tog, work in patt to the last 4 sts, ssk, k2. 2 sts decreased.

Work 1 WS row.

Rep the single dec row every RS row 7 (6, 8, 6, 4, 11, 12, 17, 18, 14) times more. 33 (35, 33, 37, 43, 37, 39, 33, 33, 33) sts. Then rep the single dec row every other RS row 3 (4, 3, 5, 6, 3, 3, 0, 0, 0) times. 27 (27, 27, 27, 31, 31, 33, 33, 33, 33) sts.

Work 1 WS row.

Double dec row (RS): K2, 2decB, work in patt to the last 5 sts, 2decF, k2. 4 sts decreased.

Rep the double dec row every RS row twice more. 15 (15, 15, 15, 19, 19, 21, 21, 21, 21) sts.

BO all sts.

FINISHING

Wash the pieces gently with wool wash, gently press out extra moisture, and lay them flat to dry.

FRONT BANDS

The airy cashmere yarn called for in this pattern doesn't provide much structure for the button-band, so a grosgrain ribbon backing is strongly recommended.

Two options are offered for using the ribbon backing.

MACHINE BUTTONHOLE METHOD

Before beginning, practice machine-sewing buttonholes on some extra grosgrain ribbon to determine the best size of buttonhole for your buttons.

Pin the grosgrain ribbon to the WS of the buttonhole band with about 2 inches/5cm extending beyond the bottom edge and 0.5 inch/ 1.5cm beyond the top edge. Lay the piece flat on a table with RS facing and the ribbon underneath the band. With a pencil, tailor's chalk, or pins, mark the center of each buttonhole on the ribbon. Remove the ribbon.

The marks on the ribbon indicate the top end of the buttonholes. Use a machine or hand-sew the buttonholes and carefully cut them open. Make sure your buttons pass through the holes before sewing the ribbon to the cardigan.

Pin the ribbon in place, lining up the buttonholes. Fold the top and bottom edges over about 0.5 inch/1.5cm and trim the excess ribbon. Using needle and thread, whipstitch all four edges of the ribbon, catching a small amount of yarn with each st, trying not to stitch through to the front of the buttonhole band.

Stitching around the buttonholes to join the ribbon to the buttonhole band is optional.

Repeat with the buttonband, omitting buttonholes and making sure that the ribbon on both bands is the same length.

SNAP METHOD

Work buttonbands on both front edges. Pin the grosgrain ribbon to the WS of the band with about 0.5 inch/1.5cm extending beyond both the top and bottom edges.

Fold the top and bottom edges over with the raw edge sandwiched between the ribbon and the band.

Using needle and thread, whipstitch all 4 edges of the ribbon, catching a small amount of yarn with each stitch, and trying not to stitch through to the front of the band.

Repeat for the other band, making sure that the ribbon is the same length on both bands.

Evenly sew buttons to the RS of the right front band. Sew snaps to the WS of the right front band behind each button. Sew matching snaps to the RS of the left front band to correspond with snaps on the right front.

BUTTONBAND

With RS facing and US #3/3.25mm needles, pick up and knit 104 (107, 110, 113, 113, 113, 116, 119, 122, 125) sts evenly along the left front edge from the neckline to the CO edge.

Inc row (WS): Pfb, p1, *k1, p2; rep from * to the last 3 sts, k1, p1, pfb. 106 (109, 112, 115, 115, 115, 118, 121, 124, 127) sts.

Row 1 (RS): Knit.

Row 2 (WS): P3, *k1, p2; rep from * to the last st, p1.

Work 4 rows more in ribbing as set, ending with a WS row.

BO in the foll patt: K3, *p1, k2; rep from * to the last st, k1.

Lightly steam the buttonband, stretching the length of the front opening, if necessary.

BUTTONHOLE BAND

Starting at bottom of the right front with RS facing, work as for the buttonband through the end of Row 2.

FOR SIZES S, M, L, XL, 2XL, 4XL, 5XL, 6XL ONLY

Row 3 (buttonhole row): Work – (6, 9, 12, 12, 12, –, 6, 9, 12) sts in rib as set, *yo, k2tog, work 10 sts; rep from * to the last 7 sts, yo, k2tog, work to the end. – (9, 9, 9, 9, 9, –, 10, 10, 10) buttonholes.

FOR SIZES XS, 3XL ONLY

Row 3 (buttonhole row): Work 6 sts in rib as set, *yo, k2tog, work 10 sts; rep from * 6 (–, –, –, –, –, 7, –, –, –) times more, yo, k2tog, work 7 sts, yo, k2tog, work to end. 9 (–, –, –, –, –, 10, –, –, –) buttonholes.

FOR ALL SIZES

Row 4: Rep Row 2.

Work 2 more rows in ribbing as set, ending with a WS row. BO in patt as for the buttonband.

Lightly steam the buttonband, stretching the length of the front opening, if necessary.

COLLAR

Sew shoulder seams, stretching the BO front shoulder edges to fit the shaped back edges.

With RS facing and US #3/3.25mm needles, pick up and knit 30 (33, 34, 32, 35, 32, 32, 34, 36, 35) sts along the right front neckline, beg at the button band seam, pm, another 33 (35, 35, 37, 37, 37, 37, 37, 39, 39) sts along the back neckline, pm, then another 30 (33, 34, 32, 35, 32, 32, 34, 36, 35) sts along the front left neckline, ending at the buttonband seam. 93 (101, 103, 101, 107, 101, 101, 105, 111, 109) sts.

FOR SIZES XS, 4XL, 5XL ONLY

Row 1 (RS collar; WS garment): Kfb, knit to the marker, k16 (–, –, –, –, –, –, 17, 18, –), k2tog, knit to the last st, kfb. 94 (–, –, –, –, –, –, 106, 112, –) sts.

FOR SIZES S, L, XL, 2XL, 3XL ONLY

Row 1 (RS collar; WS garment): Kfb, knit to the last st, kfb. – (103, –, 103, 109, 103, 103, –, –, –) sts.

FOR SIZES M, 6XL ONLY

Row 1 (RS collar; WS garment): Kfb, knit to the marker, k – (–, 18, –, –, –, –, –, –, 20), kfb, knit to the last st, kfb. – (–, 106, –, –, –, –, –, –, 112) sts.

FOR ALL SIZES

Row 2 (WS collar; RS garment): P3, *k1, p2; rep from * to the last st, p1.

SHAPE COLLAR USING SHORT ROWS

The collar is worked in mock ribbing as set (knit on RS rows; ribbing on WS rows). The German short row method is recommended; work the double strand sts together as you come to them. Feel free to substitute with your preferred short row method.

Short row 1 (RS collar; WS garment): Work to 6 sts before the second marker; turn.

Short row 2 (WS collar; RS garment): Cont in rib patt as set, work to 6 sts before the next marker; turn.

Short rows 3 and 4: Work to 4 sts before the next marker; turn.

Short rows 5 and 6: Work to 2 sts before the next marker; turn.

Short rows 7 and 8: Work to the next marker, remove the marker; turn.

Short row 9: Work to the end of the row.

Change to US #4/3.5mm needles. Work even until the collar measures 1.75 inches/4.5cm at the center back.

Change to US #5/3.75mm needles. Work even until the collar measures 2.5 inches/6.5cm at the center back.

Change to US #6/4mm needles. Work even until the collar measures 3.25 inches/8.5cm at the center back.

Change to US #7/4.5mm needles. Work even until the collar measures 4 inches/10cm at the center back, ending with a WS row.

Change to US #6/4mm needles.

Next row (RS): K2tog, knit to the last 2 sts, ssk. 92 (101, 104, 101, 107, 101, 101, 104, 110, 110) sts.

Knit 3 rows.

Using the conventional BO method, BO 18 sts, using the Russian BO method, BO to the last 18 sts, using the conventional BO method, BO rem sts.

Lay the sweater out so the collar is flat, with the BO edge curved and the neck edge straight, and lightly steam to block.

FINAL FINISHING

Place markers 2 inches/5cm down from the shoulder along the armhole edge of each front and underarm BO edges. Set in the sleeves, matching the center of the sleeve cap with markers on the fronts. Sew the sleeve and the side seams.

Weave in the ends.

RANDALL-FRASER
Sweater

Designed by Mieka John

With the fire of a Fraser and a Randall's love of history, Jamie and Claire's child, Brianna, whom Frank helped raised as his own, represents all the love, hope, and new beginnings that come with a child, and then some. When grown-up Brianna was digging up information on her Scottish roots with Roger, she wore a beautiful colorwork sweater that is as timeless as she is.

With a flattering neckline, looser fit, and three-quarter sleeves, this stylish tribute is a great match for any wardrobe. Tuck it into a long skirt and wear it with sandals on a breezy summer evening or pair it with a leather jacket, black jeans, and boots on a brisk autumn afternoon.

SKILLS REQUIRED

Working in the round, working small circumferences in the round, short rows, stranded colorwork

MATERIALS

Trendsetter Yarn Merino 6 Ply (100% superfine merino wool; 135yds/123.5m per 1.75oz/50g ball)

Sample uses the following colors:

MC: color 7126/Cocoa; 5 (5, 6, 6, 7, 7, 8) balls

CC1: color 200/Black; 2 (2, 3, 3, 4, 5, 5) balls

CC2: color 9904/Latte; 2 (2, 2, 3, 3, 4, 4) balls

Substitution Notes: A plied yarn of animal fiber in colors with high contrast will be best for achieving similar colorwork. Unless it is a small percentage in the yarn, avoid slipperier animal fibers, such as alpaca and yak, to achieve a similar drape to the yarn used in the sample.

NEEDLES

US #4/3.5mm 24-inch/60cm and 32-inch/80cm circular needles, and needles for working small circumferences in the round (standard or flexible DPNs, 1 long circular or 2 short circulars)

US #6/4mm 24-inch/60cm and 32-inch/80cm circular needles, and needles for working small circumferences in the round (standard or flexible DPNs, 1 long circular or 2 short circulars)

Or size needed to obtain gauge

NOTIONS

Stitch markers

2 stitch holders or scrap yarn for underarm stitches

Yarn needle

GAUGE

24 sts/30 rounds = 4 inches/10cm square in stockinette stitch, using larger needle

25 sts/28 rounds = 4 inches/10cm square in colorwork pattern stitch, using larger needle

24 sts/30 rounds = 4 inches/10cm square in ribbing pattern, using smaller needle

SIZES

XS (S, M, L, XL, 2XL, 3XL)

FINISHED MEASUREMENTS

Garment should be worn with 3 to 6 inches/7.5 to 15cm positive ease. Choose a size 3 to 6 inches/7.5 to 15cm larger than your upper bust/chest measurement.

A (bust circumference): 33.5 (37.5, 41.25, 46, 50, 53.75, 56.75) inches/85 (95.5, 105, 117, 127, 136.5, 144) cm

B (sleeve inseam): 12 inches/30.5cm

C (neck opening circumference): 19 (19, 19.25, 19.5, 20.5, 21, 21.25) inches/48.5 (48.5, 49, 49.5, 52, 53.5, 54) cm

D (yoke depth): 8.5 (8.75, 9.5, 10, 11, 12, 13) inches/21.5 (22, 24, 25.5, 28, 30.5, 33) cm

E (sleeve upper arm circumference): 11.5 (13.5, 13.5, 16.25, 17.25, 18.25, 19.25) inches/29 (34.5, 34.5, 41.5, 44, 46.5, 49) cm

F (sleeve cuff circumference): 9 (9, 9.25, 9.5, 10, 10.25, 10.25) inches/23 (23, 23.5, 24, 25.5, 26, 26) cm

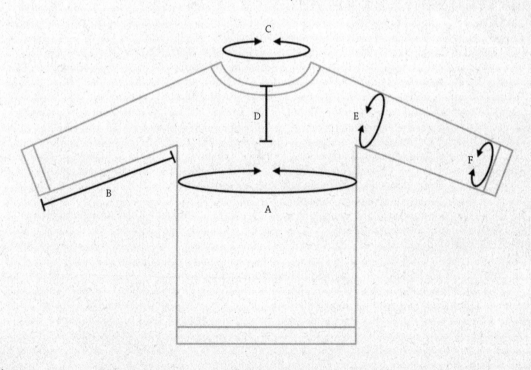

GARMENTS

CHARTS

CHART A

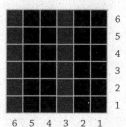

6
5
4
3
2
1

6 5 4 3 2 1

CHART B

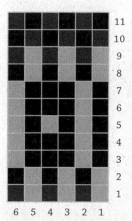

11
10
9
8
7
6
5
4
3
2
1

6 5 4 3 2 1

CHART C

4
3
2
1

2 1

PATTERN NOTES

Worked top down in the round, this sweater begins with a ribbed neckline and German short rows for shaping. The colorwork motif is introduced and worked throughout the rest of the yoke. Please note that the yoke separation into body and sleeves is worked at the same time as a round in Chart D. The sleeve stitches are put on waste yarn and the body continues until the colorwork is finished. The body is then knitted with MC in stockinette stitch with a straight body ending with a ribbed hem. The sleeve stitches are taken off waste yarn and the colorwork is worked for a short distance on the sleeves before completing in the main color.

CHART D

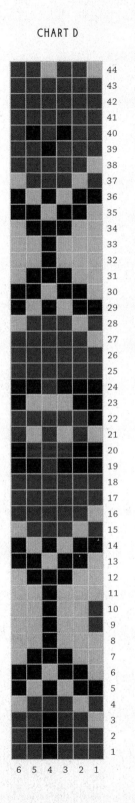

KEY

- ■ MC
- ■ CC1
- ▨ CC2

INSTRUCTIONS

YOKE

NECKLINE

With MC and shorter, smaller needle, CO 114 (114, 116, 118, 124, 126, 128) sts using the German twisted cast-on method or the cast-on method of your choice. Place BOR marker and join to work in the round, being careful not to twist.

1x1 ribbing round: *K1, p1; repeat from * to end.

Repeat the ribbing round 6 more times.

Switch to the shorter, larger needle.

Knit 1 round.

INC ROUND 1

XS: K3, (M1L, k7) 3 times, (M1L, k6) 11 times, (M1L, k7) 3 times, M1L, k3. 132 sts.

S: K3, (M1L, k5) 9 times, (M1L, k6) 3 times, (M1L, k5) 9 times, M1L, k3. 136 sts.

M: K2, (M1L, k3) 2 times, (M1L, k4) 25 times, (M1L, k3) 2 times, M1L, k2. 146 sts.

L: K1, (M1L, k3) 17 times, (M1L, k2) 7 times, (M1L, k3) 17 times, M1L, k1. 160 sts.

XL: K1, (M1L, k3) 12 times, (M1L, k2) 25 times, (M1L, k3) 12 times, M1L, k1. 174 sts.

2XL: K1, (M1L, k3) 7 times, (M1L, k2) 41 times, (M1L, k3) 7 times, M1L, k1. 182 sts.

3XL: K1, (M1L, k2) 63 times, M1L, k1. 192 sts.

Knit 1 round.

SHORT ROW SHAPING

Work the following short row shaping using the German short row method or your preferred short row method.

Short row 1 (RS): K34 (38, 40, 46, 48, 50, 54) sts, turn.

Short row 2 (WS): Purl to the BOR, sm, p34 (38, 40, 46, 48, 50, 54) sts, turn.

Short row 3: Knit to the BOR, sm, k30 (34, 36, 42, 44, 46, 48) sts, turn.

Short row 4: Purl to the BOR, sm, p30 (34, 36, 42, 44, 46, 48) sts, turn.

Short row 5: Knit to the BOR, sm, k26 (30, 32, 38, 40, 42, 44) sts, turn.

Short row 6: Purl to the BOR, sm, p26 (30, 32, 38, 40, 42, 44) sts, turn.

Short row 7: Knit to the BOR, sm, k22 (26, 28, 34, 36, 38, 40) sts, turn.

Short row 8: Purl to the BOR, sm, p22 (26, 28, 34, 36, 38, 40) sts, turn.

Knit to the BOR. Knit 1 full round, closing short row gaps as they appear in the German short row method or in your preferred short row method.

Knit 2 (2, 2, 3, 3, 4, 4) rounds.

INC ROUND 2

XS: K2, (M1L, k5) 2 times, (M1L, k4) 27 times, (M1L, k5) 2 times, M1L, k2. 164 sts.

S: K2, (M1L, k4) 33 times, M1L, k2. 170 sts.

M: K2, M1L, k5, (M1L, k4) 33 times, M1L, k5, M1L, k2. 182 sts.

L: K2, (M1L, k4) 39 times, M1L, k2. 200 sts.

XL: K2, M1L, k3, (M1L, k4) 41 times, M1L, k3, M1L, k2. 218 sts.

2XL: K2, M1L, k3, (M1L, k4) 43 times, M1L, k3, M1L, k2. 228 sts.

3XL: K2, (M1L, k4) 47 times, M1L, k2. 240 sts.

Knit 2 (2, 2, 3, 3, 4, 4) rounds.

INC ROUND 3

XS: K3, (M1L, k5) 2 times, (M1L, k6) 23 times, (M1L, k5) 2 times, M1L, k3. 192 sts.

S: K2, (M1L, k5) 33 times, M1L, k3. 204 sts.

M: K3, (M1L, k5) 11 times, (M1L, k6) 11 times, (M1L, k5) 11 times, M1L, k3. 216 sts.

L: K2, (M1L, k5) 39 times, M1L, k3. 240 sts.

XL: K2, (M1L, k5) 17 times, (M1L, k4) 11 times, (M1L, k5) 17 times, M1L, k2. 264 sts.

2XL: K3, (M1L, k5) 12 times, (M1L, k6) 17 times, (M1L, k5) 12 times, M1L, k3. 270 sts.

3XL: K2, (M1L, k5) 47 times, M1L, k3. 288 sts.

Knit 1 round.

Work Rounds 1–6 of Chart A, joining CC1 and changing to longer, larger needle when necessary.

Knit 1 round with MC.

INC ROUND 4

XS: K2, (M1L, k3) 24 times, (M1L, k4) 11 times, (M1L, k3) 24 times, M1L, k2. 252 sts.

S: K1, (M1L, k3) 24 times, (M1L, k2) 29 times, (M1L, k3) 24 times, M1L, k1. 282 sts.

M: K1, (M1L, k3) 30 times, (M1L, k2) 17 times, (M1L, k3) 30 times, M1L, k1. 294 sts.

L: K1, (M1L, k3) 18 times, (M1L, k2) 65 times, (M1L, k3) 18 times, M1L, k1. 342 sts.

XL: K1, (M1L, k3) 36 times, (M1L, k2) 23 times, (M1L, k3) 36 times, M1L, k1. 360 sts.

2XL: K1, (M1L, k3) 21 times, (M1L, k2) 71 times, (M1L, k3) 21 times, M1L, k1. 384 sts.

3XL: K1, (M1L, k3) 36 times, (M1L, k2) 35 times, (M1L, k3) 36 times, M1L, k1. 396 sts.

Work Rounds 1–11 of Chart B, joining CC1 and CC2 as needed.

Knit 1 round with MC.

INC ROUND 5

XS: K7, (M1L, k14) 17 times, M1L, k7. 270 sts.

S: K6, (M1L, k11) 3 times, (M1L, k12) 17 times, (M1L, k11) 3 times, M1L, k6. 306 sts.

M: K5, (M1L, k11) 7 times, (M1L, k10) 13 times, (M1L, k11) 7 times, M1L, k5. 322 sts.

L: K5, M1L, k11, (M1L, k10) 31 times, M1L, k11, M1L, k5. 376 sts.

XL: K6, (M1L, k11) 12 times, (M1L, k12) 7 times, (M1L, k11) 12 times, M1L, k6. 392 sts.

2XL: K5, (M1L, k11) 12 times, (M1L, k10) 11 times, (M1L, k11) 12 times, M1L, k5. 420 sts.

3XL: K6, (M1L, k11) 6 times, (M1L, k12) 21 times, (M1L, k11) 6 times, M1L, k6. 430 sts.

Work Rounds 1–4 of Chart C, joining CC1 as needed.

Knit 1 round with MC.

INC ROUND 6

XS: K4, (M1L, k7) 9 times, (M1L, k8) 17 times, (M1L, k7) 9 times, M1L, k4. 306 sts.

S: K3, (M1L, k7) 9 times, (M1L, k6) 29 times, (M1L, k7) 9 times, M1L, k3. 354 sts.

M: K3, (M1L, k5) 7 times, (M1L, k6) 41 times, (M1L, k5) 7 times, M1L, k3. 378 sts.

L: K3, (M1L, k5) 16 times, (M1L, k6) 35 times, (M1L, k5) 16 times, M1L, k3. 444 sts.

XL: K3, (M1L, k7) 4 times, (M1L, k6) 55 times, (M1L, k7) 4 times, M1L, k3. 456 sts.

2XL: K3, (M1L, k5) 12 times, (M1L, k6) 49 times, (M1L, k5) 12 times, M1L, k3. 492 sts.

3XL: K3, (M1L, k7) 11 times, (M1L, k6) 45 times, (M1L, k7) 11 times, M1L, k3. 498 sts.

Work Rounds 1–17 (19, 24, 25, 30, 35, 42) of Chart D, joining CC1 and CC2 as needed.

Measure the yoke depth from the center front. Knit as many rounds as necessary of Chart D to reach a yoke depth of 8.5 (8.75, 9.5, 10, 11, 12, 13) inches/21.5 (22, 24, 25.5, 28, 30.5, 33) cm or desired yoke depth. If Chart D is finished and the desired yoke depth is not achieved, cut CC1 and CC2 and work in stockinette stitch with MC until desired length is reached and continue in MC.

SEPARATE BODY AND SLEEVES

The following round, separating the sleeves and the body, is worked AT THE SAME TIME as the next colorwork round in Chart D. If additional rounds were not knitted to reach the target yoke depth, knit the following round, starting with Round 18 (20, 25, 26, 31, 36, 43). If additional rounds of Chart D were worked to reach the desired yoke depth, knit the following round, separating the sleeves and the body with the next round of Chart D. If additional rounds of Chart D were worked and the chart was finished, knit the following round in MC.

Next round: K47 (53, 57, 66, 69, 75, 77) back sts, slip 60 (72, 72, 90, 90, 96, 96) sleeve sts onto a stitch holder or waste yarn, CO 12 (12, 12, 12, 18, 18, 24) underarm sts using the backwards loop cast-on, k93 (105, 117, 132, 138, 150, 153) front sts, slip 60 (72, 72, 90, 90, 96, 96) sleeve sts onto a second stitch holder or waste yarn, CO 12 (12, 12, 12, 18, 18, 24) underarm sts using the backwards loop cast-on method, k46 (52, 60, 66, 69, 75, 76) back sts. 210 (234, 258, 288, 312, 336, 354) body sts on the needles.

BODY

Work the remaining rounds of Chart D until finished. Cut CC1 and CC2.

With MC, knit in stockinette stitch until the body measures 9 inches/23cm from the underarm CO edge, or 1 inch/2.5cm less than desired body length.

Switch to the shorter, smaller needles and knit 1 round. Work in 1x1 ribbing for 1 inch/2.5cm. BO using the Russian bind-off or your preferred stretchy BO method.

SLEEVES

Transfer 60 (72, 72, 90, 90, 96, 96) sts from the stitch holder or waste yarn to the larger needles for small circumferences in the round.

With RS facing, pick up and knit 6 (6, 6, 6, 9, 9, 12) sts, starting at the right corner of the underarm CO sts of the body in MC. Place the BOR marker. Pick up and knit 6 (6, 6, 6, 9, 9, 12) more sts from the underarm CO edge in MC. 72 (84, 84, 102, 108, 114, 120) sleeve sts.

Join CC1 and CC2 and work, starting with Round 18 (20, 25, 26, 31, 36, 43) in Chart D back to the BOR. Work the rem rounds of Chart D until finished. Knit 1 round in MC.

If additional rounds of Chart D were worked to reach the desired yoke depth, start with the next round of Chart D. If additional rounds of Chart D were worked for the yoke and the chart was finished, work in stockinette stitch with MC until the sleeve measures 3 inches/7.5cm from the underarm.

FOR SIZES XS, S ONLY

Finishing Chart D will be longer than 3 inches/7.5cm from the underarm. Finish Chart D, cut CC1 and CC2, knit 1 round with MC, then continue.

SLEEVE SHAPING

Begin decreases on the next round as follows:

Decrease round: K1, ssk, knit to the last 3 sts, k2tog, k1. 2 sts decreased.

Repeat the decrease round every 8 (4, 4, 2, 2, 2, 2) rounds 5 (11, 4, 5, 9, 11, 17) more times. 60 (60, 74, 90, 88, 90, 84) sts.

FOR SIZES M TO 3XL ONLY

Repeat the decrease round every – (–, 6, 4, 4, 4, 4) rounds – (–, 6, 11, 9, 8, 5) more times. 60 (60, 62, 68, 70, 74, 74) sts.

FOR ALL SIZES

Work in stockinette stitch until the sleeve measures 11 inches/28cm from the underarm, or 1 inch/2.5cm less than the desired total sleeve length.

FINAL DEC ROUND

XS: K4, (k2tog, k8) 5 times, k2tog, k4. 54 sts.

S: K4, (k2tog, k8) 5 times, k2tog, k4. 54 sts.

M: K5, (k2tog, k8) 2 times, k2tog, k9, (k2tog, k8) 2 times, k2tog, k4. 56 sts.

L: K3, k2tog, k4, (k2tog, k5) 7 times, k2tog, k4, k2tog, k2. 58 sts.

XL: K3, (k2tog, k5) 9 times, k2tog, k2. 60 sts.

2XL: K3, (k2tog, k4) 5 times, k2tog, k5, (k2tog, k4) 5 times, k2tog, k2. 62 sts.

3XL: K3, (k2tog, k4) 5 times, k2tog, k5, (k2tog, k4) 5 times, k2tog, k2. 62 sts.

Switch to smaller needles for small circumferences in the round and knit 1 round.

Work in 1x1 ribbing pattern for 1 inch/2.5cm. BO using the Russian bind-off or your preferred stretchy BO method. Repeat for the second sleeve.

FINISHING

Weave in the ends. Soak the piece and press most of the moisture out. Using blocking mats, pin to your desired shape, and leave it to dry.

JAMIE'S
Waistcoat

Designed by Jessie McKitrick

A woven or knitted vest is a practical and stylish choice to keep the body warm, but leaves the arms uncovered for ease of movement while doing farm or stable work. Everyday vests are fairly plain, but in order to make something a little special for your Jamie, this garment is embellished with trim inspired by the embroidery on the greatcoat worn by Laird Colum MacKenzie.

SKILLS REQUIRED

Working in the round, picking up stitches, seaming

MATERIALS

Trendsetter Yarns New York (100% pure organic wool; 190yds/174m per 1.75oz/50g skein); 5 (6, 7, 7, 8) skeins

Sample uses color SM013/Brown Melange.

Substitution Notes: The recommended yarn is a woolen-spun wool yarn with a two-ply structure. It is listed as a DK weight, but it is at the lighter end of the spectrum of DK yarns and some may find it more comparable to a sportweight. The yarn balances drape with elasticity and stitch definition and develops a velvety hand with a slight halo after washing. The color used in the sample is a warm, heathered medium to dark brown.

NEEDLES

US #4/3.5mm needles for working flat, 60-inch/150cm circular needle

US #2.5/3mm 16-inch/40cm circular needle

Or size needed to obtain gauge

NOTIONS

Stitch markers: 1 ring-style, 8 removable

Yarn needle

10 (11, 11, 11, 11) 0.75 inch/20mm buttons

Sewing needle and matching thread

GAUGE

23.5 sts/36 rows = 4 inches/10cm square in stockinette stitch, using the larger needle

26.5 sts/52 rounds = 4 inches/10cm square in trim pattern, worked in the round using the larger needle

SIZES

Men's S (M, L, XL, 2XL)

FINISHED MEASUREMENTS

This garment should be worn with 2 to 3 inches/
5 to 7.5cm ease. Choose a size 2 to 3 inches/
5 to 7.5cm larger than your chest (upper bust)
measurement.

Finished chest circumference of garment,
worn buttoned: 36.25 (40.25, 44.5, 48.5, 52.5)
inches/92 (102, 113, 123, 133.5) cm.

A (width of back): 18 (20, 22, 24.25, 26.25)
inches/45.5 (51, 56, 61.5, 66.5) cm

B (trim and buttonband): 1.75 inches/4.5cm

C (width of one front): 8.5 (9.5, 10.5, 11.5, 12.5)
inches/21.5 (24, 26,5, 29, 32) cm

D (neck width): 6.25 (6.25, 6.75, 6.75, 7.25)
inches/16 (16, 17, 17, 18.5) cm

E (back of neck before working trim): 9.75 (9.75,
10.25, 10.25, 11) inches/25 (25, 26, 26, 28) cm

F (shoulder width, including trim both sides): 5.25
(5.75, 6.25, 6.5, 6.75) inches/13.5 (14.5, 16, 16.5,
17) cm

G (hem to armhole, including all trim): 17 (18.5,
19, 19.5, 20) inches/43 (47, 48.5, 49.5, 51) cm

H (armhole depth): 10 (10.5, 11, 11.5, 12)
inches/25.5 (26.5, 28, 29, 30.5) cm

I (shoulder rise): 0.75 inches/2cm

J (hem to shoulder length): 27.25 (29.25, 30.25,
31.25, 32.25) inches/69 (74.5, 77, 79.5, 82) cm

K (neckline depth before working trim):
5.75 inches/14.5cm

L (neckline depth after working trim): 3.75 inches/
9.5cm

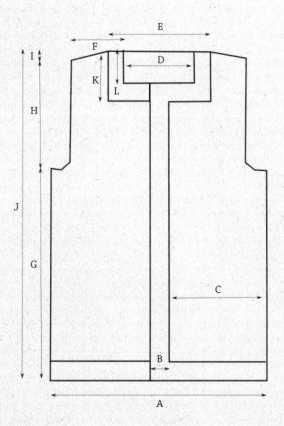

PATTERN NOTES

The back and front pieces are worked back and
forth in pieces from the bottom up and seamed.
Armholes are picked up and worked in the round.

To work the trim and buttonbands, stitches are
picked up beginning at the lower right front
side seam, up the edge of the front, around the
neckline, down the left front edge, and around
the bottom of the piece back to the right front
side seam. The trim is worked in the round, with
mitered corners that are achieved by increasing
every other round on either side of a locking stitch
marker at the outside corners and decreasing on
either side of a locking stitch marker at the inside
corners along the neckline. The stiches marked
with locking stitch markers are worked with a
knitted stitch throughout in order to set off the
corners neatly.

GARMENTS

- When picking up stitches, you may find it helpful to use additional locking stitch markers in a contrasting color or pins to help keep track of the number of stitches needed along a given section. There are a lot of stitches along the trim and buttonband, so it is worth checking frequently as you go along that you have the expected number of stitches for an area in order to avoid starting over again.

- Using different colors of locking stitch markers may be helpful in keeping track of the different corners along the trim. For instance, use one color for the corners that require increases, and use a different color for the corners that require decreases.

- When binding off the edging, check when you have bound off a good 30 stitches or so to see if your bind-off is too tight or too loose, and adjust as needed. It's a long bind-off, so best to be sure you are happy with it at an early stage!

One row of buttonholes is worked in the middle round of the trim, with the top buttonhole incorporating the increases for that round so that it fits neatly in the top corner of the edge.

MODIFICATIONS

To reduce the overall length of this waistcoat, subtract the length from the section between the cast-on edge and the armhole shaping in the back and both fronts.

SPECIAL STITCHES

Top buttonhole: Move the yarn forward, sl 1, move the yarn to the back, *sl st, pass the second st onto the right-hand needle over the first st as if to bind off; rep from * 3 more times, sl the last cast-off st from the right-hand needle back to the left-hand needle; turn. Using a cable cast-on, cast on 3 sts, cast on 1 st and mark with the locking st marker, cast on 3 sts. Turn work. Sl 1, pass the second st onto the right-hand needle over the first st as if to bind off.

Each additional buttonhole: Move the yarn forward, sl 1, move the yarn to the back, *sl st, pass the second st on the right-hand needle over the first st as if to bind off; rep from * 3 more times, sl the last cast-off st from the right-hand needle back to the left-hand needle; turn. Using a cable cast-on, cast on 5 sts. Turn work. Sl 1, pass the second st onto the right-hand needle over the first st as if to bind off.

~~~~~~~~~~~~~~~~~~~~~~~~~~~~

INSTRUCTIONS

BACK

Using larger needles, cast on 108 (120, 132, 144, 156) sts. Work in St st until the work measures 14.5 (16, 16.5, 17, 17.5) inches/37 (40.5, 42, 43, 44.5) cm from cast-on edge, ending with a WS row.

SHAPE ARMHOLES

Bind off 4 (6, 8, 10, 12) sts at the beg of the next 2 rows, then 2 sts at the beg of the foll 2 (2, 2, 4, 4) rows. 96 (104, 112, 116, 124) sts.

Dec row (RS): K1, ssk, work to last 3 sts, k2tog, k1. 2 sts decreased.

Rep dec row every RS row 1 (3, 3, 4, 4) more time(s). 92 (96, 104, 106, 114) sts.

Work even until the armhole measures 9 (9.5, 10, 10.5, 11) inches/23 (24, 25.5, 26.5, 28) cm, ending with a WS row.

SHAPE BACK OF NECK AND SHOULDERS

Next row (RS): K17 (19, 22, 23, 25) sts, bind off the foll 58 (58, 60, 60, 64) sts, knit to the end. 17 (19, 22, 23, 25) sts rem for each shoulder.

Work the left back shoulder even until the work measures 1 inch/2.5cm from the back of neck shaping, ending with a RS row. Bind off 6 (6, 7, 8, 8) sts at the beg of the next 2 WS rows, then, on the foll WS row, bind off the rem sts in pattern.

Beg with a WS row, join the yarn at the neckline edge to work the right back shoulder. Work even until the work measures 1 inch/2.5cm from the back of neck shaping, ending with a WS row. Bind off 6 (6, 7, 8, 8) sts at the beg of the next 2 RS rows, then, on the foll RS row, bind off the rem sts in pattern.

RIGHT FRONT

Using larger needle, cast on 52 (58, 64, 70, 76) sts. Work in St st until the work measures 14.5 (16, 16.5, 17, 17.5) inches/37 (40.5, 42, 43, 44.5) cm from the cast-on edge, ending with a WS row.

SHAPE ARMHOLES

Bind off 4 (6, 8, 10, 12) sts at the beg of the next row, then 2 sts at the beg of the foll 1 (1, 1, 2, 2) RS row(s). 46 (50, 54, 56, 60) sts.

Work 1 WS row.

Dec row (RS): K1, ssk, work to the end. 1 st decreased.

Rep dec row every RS row 1 (3, 3, 4, 4) more time(s). 44 (46, 50, 51, 55) sts

Work even until the armhole measures 5 (5.5, 6, 6.5, 7) inches/12.5 (14, 15, 16.5, 18) cm, ending with a WS row.

SHAPE NECKLINE

Next row (RS): Bind off 27 (27, 28, 28, 30) sts, work to the end. 17 (19, 22, 23, 25) sts.

Work even until the armhole measures 10 (10.5, 11, 11.5, 12) inches/25.5 (26.5, 28, 29, 30.5) cm, ending with a RS row.

SHAPE SHOULDER

Bind off 6 (6, 7, 8, 8) sts at the beg of the next 2 WS rows, then, on the foll WS row, bind off the rem sts in pattern.

LEFT FRONT

Work as for the right front up to Shape Armholes.

SHAPE ARMHOLES

Work 1 RS row.

Bind off 4 (6, 8, 10, 12) sts at the beg of the next WS row, then 2 sts at the beg of the foll 1 (1, 1, 2, 2) WS row(s). 46 (50, 54, 56, 60) sts.

Dec row (RS): K1, work to the last 3 sts, k2tog, k1. 1 st decreased.

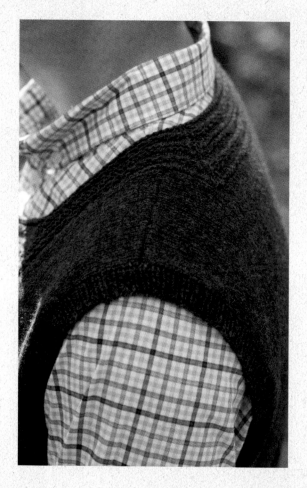

Rep dec row every RS row 1 (3, 3, 4, 4) more time(s). 44 (46, 50, 51, 55) sts.

Work even until the armhole measures 5 (5.5, 6, 6.5, 7) inches/12.5 (14, 15, 16.5, 18) cm, ending with a RS row.

SHAPE NECKLINE

Next row (WS): Bind off 27 (27, 28, 28, 30) sts, work to the end. 17 (19, 22, 23, 25) sts.

Work even until the armhole measures 10 (10.5, 11, 11.5, 12) inches/25.5 (26.5, 28, 29, 30.5) cm, ending with a WS row.

SHAPE SHOULDER

Bind off 6 (6, 7, 8, 8) sts at the beg of the next 2 RS rows, then, on the foll RS row, bind off the rem sts in pattern.

FINISHING

Wash the pieces gently with wool wash, gently press out extra moisture, and lay them flat to dry. Seam the shoulders and the side seams.

ARMHOLES

With RS facing and using the smaller short circular needles, and beg at the lower edge of the armhole at the side seam, pick up and knit 8 (13, 14, 20, 22) sts along the armhole shaping, pick up and knit 114 (116, 120, 122, 128) sts along the straight edge of the armhole to the armhole shaping, pick up and knit 8 (13, 14, 20, 22) sts along the rem edge of the armhole. 130 (142, 148, 162, 172) sts.

Pm and join to work in the round, being careful not to twist.

Next round: *K1, p1; rep from* to the end.

Rep the last round 6 more times. Bind off all sts. Rep on the other side.

TRIM AND BUTTONBAND

Using the long circular needle, and beg at the bottom of the right front at the side seam, pick up and knit 51 (57, 63, 69, 75) sts along the lower edge of the right front, pick up and knit 1 st at the corner edge and mark with a locking st marker, pick up and knit 131 (147, 151, 158, 165) sts along the right front edge, pick up and knit 1 st at the corner edge and mark with a locking st marker, pick up and knit 27 (27, 28, 28, 30) sts along the right front neckline, pick up and knit 1 st at the corner edge and mark with a locking st marker, pick up and knit 46 sts along the shoulder neckline edge, pick up and knit 1 st at the corner edge and mark with a locking st marker, pick up and knit 58 (58, 60, 60, 64) sts along the back of the neck, pick up and knit 1 st at the corner edge and mark with a locking st marker, pick up and knit 46 sts along the shoulder neckline edge, pick up and knit 1 st at the corner edge and mark with a locking st marker, pick up and knit 27 (27, 28, 28, 30) sts along the left front neckline, pick up and knit 1 st at corner edge and mark with a locking st marker, pick up and knit 131 (147, 151, 158, 165) sts along the left front edge, pick up and knit 1 st at corner edge and mark with a locking st marker, pick up and knit 158 (176, 194, 212, 230) sts along the bottom of the left front and back. 663 (739, 775, 813, 859) sts.

Pm and join to work in the round.

Note: Work the st marked with the locking st marker as a knitted stitch throughout the edging. Move the locking st marker up along the same st column as the work progresses.

Round 1: *Purl to the locking st marker, k1; rep from * 7 more times, purl to the end.

Round 2: *Knit to the locking st marker, m1, k1, m1; rep from * one more time, * knit to 2 sts before the locking st marker, ssk, k1, k2tog; rep from * 3 more times, * knit to the locking st marker, m1, k1, m1; rep from * one more time, knit to the end.

Round 3: Knit to the end.

Round 4: Rep Round 2.

Round 5: *P1, sl 1; work in patt as set from * to 1 st before the locking st marker, p1, k1; rep from * to end, working all the sts that are marked with the locking st marker as a knitted stitch.

Round 6: *Sl 1, p1; work in patt as set from * to the locking st marker, m1p, k1, m1p; rep from * one more time, *sl 1, p1; work in patt as set from * to 2 sts before the locking st marker, p2tog, k1, p2tog; rep from * 3 more times, *sl 1, p1; work in patt as set from * to the locking st marker, m1p, k1, m1p; rep from * one more time, *sl 1, p1; work in patt as set from * to end.

Round 7: Rep Round 5.

Rounds 8–10: Rep Rounds 2–4.

Round 11: Rep Round 1.

Round 12: *Knit to the locking st marker, m1, k1, m1; rep from * one more time, * knit to 2 sts before the locking st marker, ssk, k1, k2tog; rep from * 3 more times, knit to 2 sts before the locking st marker, make the top buttonhole (see Special Stitches), * k10 (10, 10, 11, 11) sts, make the buttonhole (see Special Stitches); rep from * 8 (9, 9, 9, 9) more times, knit to the locking st marker, m1, k1, m1, knit to the end.

Round 13: Rep Round 1.

Rounds 14–16: Rep Rounds 2–4.

Rounds 17–19: Rep Rounds 5–7.

Rounds 20–22: Rep Rounds 2–4.

Bind off all sts in reverse St st.

Wash gently with wool wash, gently press out the extra moisture, and lay it flat to dry. To align the garment when laying it out to dry, take care that the garment is folded neatly at the shoulder seams and side seams; that will be a help. Gently pat the trim into place; it should settle nicely into place, but some light pinning along the edges of the trim can help encourage it to lie flat. Weave in the ends. With matching sewing thread, sew on the buttons opposite the buttonholes.

SEASON
1

EPISODE
9

Dyeing Wool
AND THAT SCENE IN "RENT"

⬡⬡⬡⬡⬡⬡⬡⬡

Even if you've only seen it once, you likely remember that scene in episode 5 of season 1, titled "Rent," in which Claire is told to pee in a bucket. This scene is funny, charming, and historically accurate, right down to the song the women are singing. The women are treating a length of handwoven wool fabric to prepare it for being made into clothes. The urine is used to set the dye; what they're doing on the table is called "waulking" the wool. The wet wool is being massaged and beaten, so that it will shrink and thicken, becoming dense and windproof, to handle the harshest of Highlands weather.

The traditional songs help to pass the time and keep the rhythm, as the process would often take a while. There was a rich tradition of these types of songs—some slow and serious, others fast and light—being adapted and changed on the fly to suit the time required for a given piece of cloth. Modern weavers and knitters are more likely to use a washing machine for this process, but it can still be done by hand. Using a bucket of warm water and a toilet bowl plunger is a very effective way to achieve the same effect, especially if you don't have all your neighbors nearby to help.

As for the urine, the ammonia in it acted as a mordant, which helps dye bind to wool fibers, making the colors brighter and making them last longer.

Modern dyers use straight ammonia (or other chemical compounds), which is much more sanitary. And if you find that the color is running in your yarn—not uncommon with dark or bright colors like red—adding a little white vinegar to the rinse water can help. Use about one tablespoon per cup of water. This process doesn't work for cotton or other fibers—there's a surprising amount of chemistry involved in dyeing.

LIBRARY
Vest

Designed by Anthea Willis

The Library Vest is a simple cabled slipover in a style popularized in the 1940s as part of a versatile twin set. In episode 1 of season 2, Claire, wearing her cabled vest with a blouse and a pencil skirt, realizes that she must leave Jamie and the past behind and raise her unborn baby with Frank.

Soft and slightly tweedy wool yarn produces a warm, cozy fabric with traditional staghorn cables, evocative of the Scottish stags that roam among the heather-clad hills. Designed to fit closely, it can be worn alone or with a blouse or shirt underneath for Claire's classic 1940s look.

SKILLS REQUIRED

Working small circumferences in the round on DPNs, with magic loop, or with two circulars; working from charts; cables; picking up stitches; seaming

MATERIALS

Trendsetter Yarn New York (100% organic merino; 180yds/165m per 1.75oz/50g skein); 3 (3, 4, 4, 5, 5) skeins

Sample uses color 90010/Cream Melange.

Substitution Notes: A woolen-spun, plied yarn with high wool content in sportweight or light DK will give a finish very much like the sample. Trendsetter's New York has a very subtle tweedy texture and darker flecks in the cream, which gives a natural undyed look. This pattern will work best with a solid color to allow the cables to stand out!

NEEDLES

US #3/3.25mm needles for working flat

US #3/3.25mm needles for working small circumferences in the round (standard or flexible DPNs, 1 long circular or 2 short circulars)

US #5/3.75mm needles for working flat

Or size needed to obtain gauge

NOTIONS

Cable needle

2 stitch holders or scrap yarn for neck stitches

Yarn needle

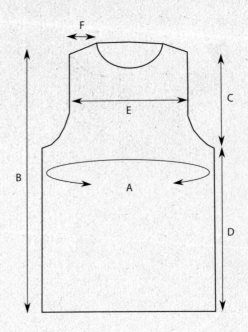

GAUGE

22 sts/36 rows = 4 inches/10cm square in stockinette stitch using larger needles

23 sts/36 rows = 4 inches/10cm square in cable pattern using larger needles

SIZES

XS (S, M, L, XL, 2XL, 3XL)

FINISHED MEASUREMENTS

This garment should be worn with 0 to 2 inches/0 to 5cm negative ease. Choose a size 0 to 2 inches/0 to 5cm smaller than your upper bust/chest measurement.

A (bust circumference): 28 (32, 36, 40, 44, 48, 52) inches/71 (81.5, 91.5, 101.5, 112, 122, 132) cm

B (length): 21 (21.5, 22.25, 22.75, 23.5, 24.75, 25.25) inches/53.5 (54.5, 56.5, 58, 59.5, 63, 64) cm

C (armhole depth): 6.5 (7, 7.75, 8.25, 9, 9.25, 9.75) inches/16.5 (18, 19.5, 21, 23, 23.5, 25) cm

D (body length to underarm): 13.5 (13.5, 13.5, 13.5, 13.5, 14.5, 14.5) inches/34.5 (34.5, 34.5, 34.5, 34.5, 37, 37) cm

E (back width above armholes): 12.25 (13.25, 14, 15.75, 17, 18, 19.75) inches/31 (33.5, 35.5. 40, 43, 45.5, 50) cm

F (shoulder width): 4.25 (4.5, 4.75, 5.5, 5.75, 6.25, 7) inches/11 (11.5, 12, 14, 14.5, 16, 18) cm

PATTERN NOTES

The Library Vest is knitted flat in two pieces from the bottom up. Shoulders and sides are seamed, then stitches are picked up around the armholes for a rib band worked in the round. Stitches are picked up along the neck for the neck band rib, which is also worked in the round.

MODIFICATIONS

The pattern is designed to be fitted, but the cable pattern is quite stretchy so there is a bit of leeway between sizes. If your bust measurement is between sizes, going up or down will produce a looser or more fitted look. If in doubt, use the armhole depth measurement to determine which size will fit the most comfortably. Length can easily be added to the body if required but remember to include the added length to the measurements when determining where to begin neck/shoulder shaping!

CABLE PANEL (over 16 stitches)

Work from the chart or the written instructions, whichever you prefer.

Row 1 (RS): P1, k1 tbl, p1, k2, C3B, C3F, p1, k2, k1 tbl, p1.

Rows 2, 4, and 6 (WS): K1, p1 tbl, k1, p10, k1, p1 tbl, k1.

Row 3: P1, k1 tbl, p1, k1, C3B, k2, C3F, k1, p1, k1 tbl, p1.

Row 5: P1, k1 tbl, p1, C3B, k4, C3F, p1, k1 tbl, p1.

SPECIAL STITCHES

C3B: Slip the next stitch onto the cable needle and hold at the back of the work, knit the next 2 sts, then knit the stitch off the cable needle.

C3F: Slip the next 2 sts onto the cable needle and hold in front of the work, knit the next stitch then knit the 2 stitches off the cable needle.

~~~~~~~~~~~~~~~~~~~~~~~~~~~~~~~~

INSTRUCTIONS

BACK

With smaller needles, CO 83 (93, 105, 115, 125, 137, 147) sts.

Row 1 (RS): *K1, p1; rep from * to the last st, k1.

Row 2 (WS): *P1, k1; rep from * to the last st, p1.

Repeat Rows 1–2 ten more times, or until rib measures 2.5 inches/6.5cm.

Change to larger needles.

Setup row (RS): K12 (16, 20, 23, 26, 30, 33), work Row 1 of the Cable Panel, k5 (6, 8, 10, 12, 14, 16), work Row 1 of the Cable Panel, k5 (6, 8, 10, 12, 14, 16), work Row 1 of the Cable Panel, knit to 3 sts before the end of the row, ssk, k1. 82 (92, 104, 114, 124, 136, 146) sts.

CABLE PANEL

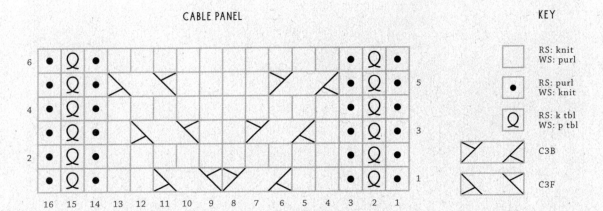

KEY

☐	RS: knit / WS: purl
•	RS: purl / WS: knit
Ω	RS: k tbl / WS: p tbl
✕	C3B
✕	C3F

Row 2 (WS): P12 (16, 20, 23, 26, 30, 33), work Row 2 of the Cable Panel, p5 (6, 8, 10, 12, 14, 16), work Row 2 of the Cable Panel, p5 (6, 8, 10, 12, 14, 16), work Row 2 of the Cable Panel, purl to the end of the row.

Row 3: K12 (16, 20, 23, 26, 30, 33) work the next row of the Cable Panel, k5 (6, 8, 10, 12, 14, 16), work the next row of the Cable Panel, k5 (6, 8, 10, 12, 14, 16), work the next row of the Cable Panel, knit to the end of the row.

Row 4: P12 (16, 20, 23, 26, 30, 33), work the next row of the Cable Panel, p5 (6, 8, 10, 12, 14, 16), work the next row of the Cable Panel, p5 (6, 8, 10, 12, 14, 16), work the next row of the Cable Panel, purl to the end of the row.

Rep Rows 3 and 4 until the back measures approximately 13.5 (13.5, 13.5, 13.5, 13.5, 14.5, 14.5) inches/34.5 (34.5, 34.5, 34.5, 34.5, 37, 37) cm from the cast-on edge, ending with a WS row.

ARMHOLE SHAPING

BO 4 (4, 5, 6, 7, 8, 8) sts at the beg of the next 4 rows. 66 (76, 84, 90, 96, 104, 114) sts rem.

Next row (RS): K1, ssk, work in patt to the last 3 sts, k2tog, k1.

> • When shaping the armholes on some sizes you may find that you are decreasing into the cable panel. For ease when picking up the stitches for the armband later, make sure that you knit the 2 stitches at the armhole edge, then continue the cable panel as set. The same applies at the shoulders—just work the parts of the cable that you can and knit the remaining stitches in stockinette stitch (k on RS, p on WS).

Next row (WS): Work in patt to the end of the row.

Rep the last 2 rows 4 (6, 8, 6, 6, 7, 5) more times. 56 (62, 66, 76, 82, 88, 98) sts rem.

Cont straight until the work measures 20 (21.5, 21.25, 21.75, 22.5, 22.75, 23.25) inches/51 (54.5, 54, 55, 57, 58, 59) cm, ending with a WS row.

SHOULDER AND NECK SHAPING

LEFT SHOULDER AND NECK

Row 1 (RS): BO 3 (4, 4, 5, 6, 5, 5) sts, work the next 12 (13, 14, 18, 19, 23, 27) sts in patt, turn. 13 (14, 15, 19, 20, 24, 28) sts.

Row 2 (WS): BO 1 st, work to the end of the row. 12 (13, 14, 18, 19, 23, 27) sts.

Row 3: BO 3 (4, 4, 5, 6, 5, 6) sts, work to the end of the row. 9 (9, 10, 13, 13, 18, 21) sts.

Row 4: BO 1 st, work to the end of the row. 8 (8, 9, 12, 12, 17, 20) sts.

Row 5: BO 4 (4, 4, 6, 6, 5, 6) sts, work to the end of the row. 4 (4, 5, 6, 6, 12, 14) sts

Row 6: Work as set to the end of the row.

FOR SIZES XS, S, M, L, XL ONLY

Row 7: BO rem 4 (4, 5, 6, 6) sts.

FOR SIZES 2XL, 3XL ONLY

Row 7: BO 6 (7) sts, work to the end.

Row 8: Work as set to the end of the row.

Row 9: BO rem 6 (7) sts.

Place the center 24 (26, 28, 28, 30, 30, 32) sts on a holder and rejoin the yarn.

Work 1 row on the rem 16 (18, 19, 24, 26, 29, 33) sts.

Next row (WS): BO 3 (3, 4, 5, 6, 5, 5) sts, work to the end of the row. 13 (14, 15, 19, 20, 24, 28) sts.

Row 2 (RS): BO 1 st, work to the end of the row. 12 (13, 14, 18, 19, 23, 27) sts.

Row 3: BO 3 (4, 4, 5, 6, 5, 6) sts, work to the end of the row. 9 (9, 10, 13, 13, 18, 21) sts.

Row 4: BO 1 st, work to the end of the row. 8 (8, 9, 12, 12, 17, 20) sts.

Row 5: BO 4 (4, 4, 6, 6, 5, 6) sts, work to the end of the row. 4 (4, 5, 6, 6, 12, 14) sts.

Row 6: Work as set to the end of the row.

FOR SIZES XS, S, M, L, XL ONLY

Row 7: BO rem 4 (4, 5, 6, 6) sts.

FOR SIZES 2XL, 3XL ONLY

Row 7: BO 6 (7) sts, work to the end of the row. 6 (7) sts.

Row 8: Work as set to the end of the row.

Row 9: BO the rem 6 (7) sts.

FRONT

Work as for the back to the end of the armhole shaping. Cont in patt until the work measures 19 (19.5, 20.25, 20.75, 21.5, 21.75, 22.25) inches/48.5 (49.5, 51.5, 52.5, 54.5, 55, 56.5) cm from the cast-on edge.

NECK AND SHOULDER SHAPING

FOR ALL SIZES

Next row (RS): Work 21(23, 25, 30, 32, 35, 40) sts in patt, turn.

FOR SIZES XS, S, M, L, XL ONLY

BO 2 sts at the beg of the next 2 WS rows, then BO 1 st at the beg of the following 3 WS rows. 14 (16, 18, 23, 25) sts rem.

FOR SIZES 2XL, 3XL ONLY

BO 2 sts at the beg of the next 4 WS rows. 27 (32) sts rem.

SHOULDER SHAPING (FOR ALL SIZES)

Next row (RS): BO 3 (4, 4, 5, 6, 5, 6) sts, work to the end of the row. 11 (12, 14, 18, 19, 22, 26) sts.

Row 2 (and all WS rows): Work in patt to the end.

Row 3: BO 3 (4, 4, 5, 6, 5, 6) sts, work to the end of the row. 8 (8, 10, 13, 13, 17, 20) sts.

Row 5: BO 4 (4, 4, 6, 6, 5, 6) sts, work to the end of the row. 4 (4, 6, 7, 7, 12, 14) sts.

FOR SIZES XS, S, M, L, XL ONLY

Row 7: BO rem 4 (4, 6, 7, 7) sts.

FOR SIZES 2X, 3X ONLY

Row 7: BO 6 (7) sts, work to the end of the row. 6 (7) sts.

Row 9: BO rem 6 (7) sts.

FOR ALL SIZES

Place the next 14 (16, 16, 16, 18, 18, 18) sts onto a holder and rejoin the yarn.

Work 2 rows on the rem 21 (23, 25, 30, 32, 35, 40) sts.

FOR SIZES XS, S, M, L, XL ONLY

BO 2 sts at the beginning of the next 2 RS rows, then BO 1 st at the beg of the following 3 RS rows. 14 (16, 18, 23, 25) sts rem.

FOR SIZES 2XL, 3XL ONLY

BO 2 (3) sts at the beg of the next RS row, then BO 2 sts at the beg of the following 3 RS rows. 27 (32) sts rem.

SHOULDER SHAPING (FOR ALL SIZES)

Next row (WS): BO 3 (4, 4, 5, 6, 5, 6) sts, work to the end of the row. 11 (12, 14, 18, 19, 22, 26) sts.

Row 2 (and all RS rows): Work in patt.

Row 3: BO 3 (4, 4, 5, 6, 5, 6) sts, work to the end of the row. 8 (8, 10, 13, 13, 17, 20) sts.

Row 5: BO 4 (4, 4, 6, 6, 5, 6) sts, work to the end of the row. 4 (4, 6, 7, 7, 12, 14) sts.

FOR SIZES XS, S, M, L, XL ONLY

Row 7: BO remaining 4 (4, 6, 7, 7) sts

FOR SIZES 2XL, 3XL ONLY

Row 7: BO 6 (7) sts, work to the end of the row. 6 (7) sts.

Row 9: BO the rem 6 (7) sts.

FINISHING

Wash the pieces gently with wool wash, gently press out extra moisture, and lay them flat to dry. Join the front and back pieces together at the shoulders and side seams, using mattress stitch.

ARMHOLE EDGING

With RS facing, starting at the center underarm and using the US #3/3.25mm needles for working small circumferences in the round, rejoin the yarn and pick up and knit 96 (98, 114, 124, 128, 138, 142) sts evenly around the armhole and join to knit in the round.

Round 1: *K1, p1; repeat from * to the end.

Repeat Round 1 eight more times. BO loosely in rib.

Repeat for the second armhole band.

NECK EDGING

With RS facing, using the smaller needles for working small circumferences in the round, and starting at the left shoulder seam, pick up and knit 16 (16, 16, 16, 16, 19, 19) sts to the held sts at the front neck, knit across 14 (16, 16, 16, 18, 18, 18) sts on the holder, pick up and knit 16 (16, 16, 16, 16, 19, 19) sts to the right shoulder seam and 6 (6, 6, 6, 7, 7, 7) sts down the back neck shaping, knit across 24 (26, 28, 28, 30, 30, 32) sts from the holder and pick up and knit 6 (6, 6, 6, 7, 7, 7) sts to the left shoulder seam. 82 (86, 88, 88, 94, 100, 102) sts.

Join to knit in the round.

Round 1: *K1, p1; rep from * to the end.

Repeat Round 1 eight more times. BO off loosely in rib.

Weave in the ends. Soak the finished vest in warm water, gently squeeze out excess water, and lay it out flat to dry, gently pulling it to desired dimensions as shown on the schematic.

REVIRESCIT
Tea Cozy

Designed by Anne Blayney

This tea cozy plays with some of the symbols of the Jacobite movement, in which Claire and Jamie are reluctantly but inextricably caught up. One of the most common symbols of the movement was the oak leaf and acorns. The oak had long been a symbol of the Stuarts, and of the Restoration. Charles II (brother and predecessor of Bonnie Prince Charlie's grandfathers James II and VII) reportedly hid in an oak tree at Boscobel House during the English Civil War, which became famous as "The Royal Oak," namesake of many ships, pubs, songs, and tales.

During the Jacobite movement, the image of withered or autumnal oak leaves was often accompanied by the Latin motto "revirescit," which means "revives." This symbol of restoration and regeneration had obvious significance to those hoping to restore the Stuarts to the throne, and yet, like most subversive symbols, it could easily be explained away as benign.

This cozy is worked in the round, using the stranded colorwork technique.

SKILLS REQUIRED

Working small circumferences in the round on DPNs, with magic loop, or with two circulars; working from charts; stranded colorwork

MATERIALS

Trendsetter Yarns Wish (75% organic wool, 25% polyamide; 165 yds/150m per 1.75 oz/50g skein)

Sample uses the following colors:

MC: color 129/Charcoal; 1 skein

CC: color 162/Honey; 1 skein

Substitution Notes: A wooly DK weight yarn with plenty of loft to create effective insulation is key here. It does not need to be next-to-the-skin soft. The background color is dark (to camouflage tea stains!) and the contrast color can be golden-brown, like aging oak leaves, or perhaps a vibrant spring green to represent regrowth. Trendsetter Yarns Wish is also gently heathered and tweedy, which adds a traditional flavor; this pattern is best suited to solid or heathered colors, rather than tonal or multitonal yarns.

NEEDLES

US #4/3.5mm 16-inch/40cm circular needles

US #6/4mm 16-inch/40cm circular needles

Or size needed to obtain gauge

A spare needle of a similar size for the closure

NOTION

Yarn needle

GAUGE

19 sts/30 rounds = 4 inches/10cm square in stockinette stitch, using US #6/4mm needles

23 sts/27 rounds = 4 inches/10cm square in pattern stitch using US #6/4mm needles

SIZES

4-cup teapot (6-cup teapot)

FINISHED MEASUREMENTS

Height: 7.5 (8) inches/19 (20.5) cm

Circumference at hem: 23 (29.5) inches/58.5 (75) cm

TIPS

- As with any figurative motif in stranded knitting, there are some unavoidable long runs of a single color. For up to 4 stitches of a single color, basic stranded knitting is fine; for runs of 5 or more stitches, it is important to catch the unused strand on the inside of the work to avoid long floats that will catch. Be sure to keep floats relaxed or the finished knitting will have a tendency to pucker. Some knitters prefer to do colorwork inside-out in order to keep the floats loose; experiment and see what works best for you.

Note: The cozy covers the handle and spout entirely, so measure the total circumference of the pot, including those protrusions.

PATTERN NOTES

The cozy is worked in the round, using the stranded colorwork technique. Wedge-shaped gussets sport the acorns, while the main panels feature the oak leaves, with a subtle tartan effect in the background that helps to prevent the long floats that would otherwise cause catching or puckering in the knitting. Ribbing at the bottom snugs the cozy in and keeps the edge from rolling.

MODIFICATIONS

- The shape of the cozy is meant to accommodate the traditional Brown Betty teapot in 4- and 6-cup sizes, but teapots are endlessly varied. There are two versions of Chart A, one for a 4-cup pot, one for a 6-cup pot.
- For taller or shorter pots, the length of the ribbing at the bottom can be adjusted; for

smaller pots, the gusset (Chart B) can be eliminated; and for larger ones, the gusset (including the vertical stripes that define it) can be made thicker. The weight and gauge of the yarn will also impact the finished size; worked in lace weight on the tiniest sock needles, this could be an egg cozy rather than a tea cozy! Changes in gauge will, of course, impact the yardage required.

CHARTS

CHART A (SIZE S)

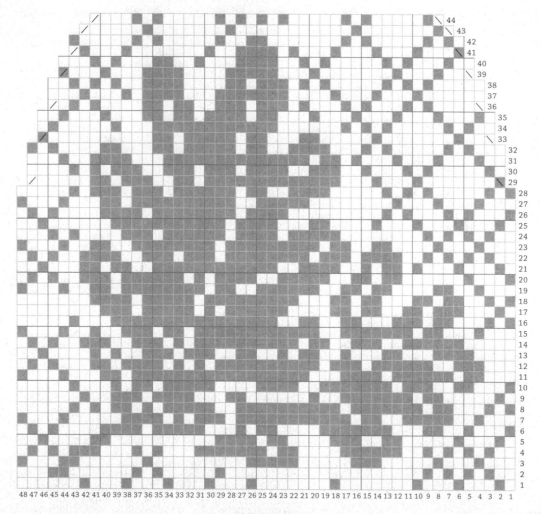

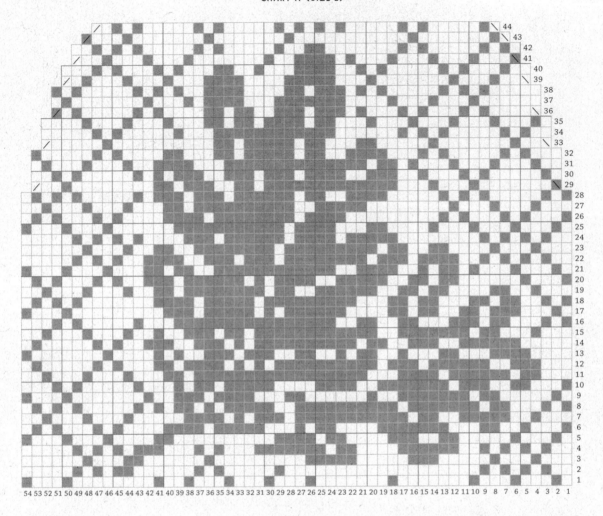

INSTRUCTIONS

LOWER EDGE

Using CC yarn and smaller needles, cast on 130 (142) sts. Place marker and join for working in the round, being careful not to twist.

Ribbing round: (K1, p1) around.

Work ribbing as set for 5 (9) rounds total.

Next round: Knit around. (This prevents the purl bumps of the ribbing from showing up as flecks in the colorwork.)

BODY

Switch to the larger needles. Join MC.

Body round: (Work Chart A [for appropriate size], work Chart B) twice.

Work as set until the charts are complete. Break MC. 76 (88) sts rem.

CHART B

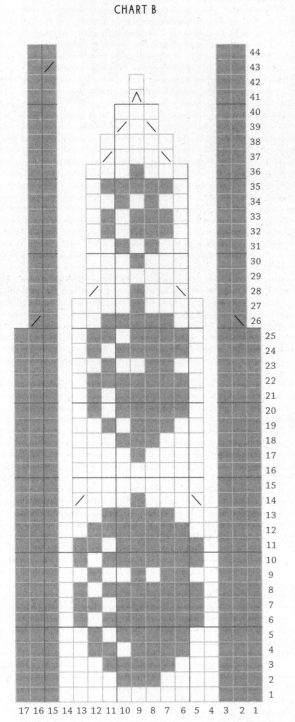

KEY

- ☐ MC
- ▨ CC
- ╱ k2tog
- ╲ ssk
- ⋀ sl 1, k2tog, psso

With CC, knit around to 2 sts before the end. This is the new start of the round. Rearrange the stitches on the needles in preparation for the three-needle bind-off. Make sure that there are 38 (44) stitches apiece on the front needle and the back needle. Using a third needle (the smaller one used for the ribbing is fine), work the three-needle bind-off.

FINISHING

Weave in the ends, wash gently with a wool wash, press most of the moisture out, and lay flat to dry. Fold the tea cozy along one set of the corners, and when it's partly dry, refold it along the other set of corners so that all four corners have a crease. If you use blocking pins, you can fold the gussets in like an expanding file, and create the crease in all four corners at once, but the four layers of fabric at the sides will make it slower to dry.

SEASON
1

EPISODE
1

MO CHRIDHE
Baby Blanket

Designed by Lynne Sosnowski

What better way to celebrate a new wee bairn than to wrap him or her in their own tartan? The Clan MacKenzie tartan inspired the color choices, though they've been brightened for the modern nursery.

The blanket is formed of easy knit and purl stitches, where horizontal color changes and vertical textures combine to give the overall impression of a plaid. A sumptuous but easy-care, hand-dyed yarn is used here in a superwash base, in hopes that Mo Chridhe becomes a favorite and needs regular laundering. If your beloved bairn is not so wee, instructions are also given for a throw size.

SKILLS REQUIRED

Provisional cast-on, Kitchener stitch/grafting

MATERIALS

Sweet Georgia Superwash DK (100% superwash merino wool; 256 yds/234m per 4oz/115g skein)

Sample uses the following colors:

MC: color Bison; 2 (5) skeins—note that for the crib size nearly all of 2 skeins is used; a third skein is recommended for insurance

CC1: color Tumbled Stone; 2 (4) skeins

CC2: color Summer Skin; 1 (1) skein

Substitution Notes: Choose a smooth double-knitting (DK) weight yarn with a bouncy hand and good stretch recovery. A wool or wool-blend yarn is recommended for the best insulation, durability, and fire retardation. If easy care or frequent launderings are desirable, a superwash wool blend is ideal.

Because this project uses light and dark colors together, it is wise to test your yarns for color-fastness before beginning. To do this, soak a short length of yarn in water until fully saturated, and then wrap it around a piece of paper towel. If the color runs onto the paper, then the yarn won't be colorfast in washing.

NEEDLES

US #6/4mm needles for working flat—a long circular needle is recommended

Or size needed to obtain gauge

NOTIONS

Approximately 2 (4) yds/1.5 (3) m of fingering or DK waste yarn in a clearly contrasting color

Crochet hook, size US #4/3.5mm or US #6/4mm

Safety pin or locking stitch marker

Stitch markers: 8 (12) of one color at minimum, indicated as marker A; an additional 36 (54) in a different color may prove helpful

Yarn needle

GAUGE

21 sts/30 rows = 4 inches/10cm square in stockinette stitch

20 sts/28 rows = 4 inches/10cm square in pattern stitch

SIZES

Crib Blanket (Throw)

FINISHED MEASUREMENTS

Width: 30 (46) inches/76 (117) cm

Height: 36 (54) inches/91 (137) cm

PATTERN NOTES

Mo Chridhe is worked by provisionally casting on enough stitches for the desired width, and then working the pattern in the given stripe sequence to the desired height. An I-cord edge is then worked around the whole blanket, first across the live stitches at the top, along picked-up stitches on one side, on the provisionally cast-on stitches at the bottom, and then again along the picked-up stitches on the remaining side. The few stitches at the beginning and ending of the cord are then grafted together using Kitchener stitch.

INSTRUCTIONS

The first number given is for the Crib Blanket size; the number in parentheses is for the Throw size.

TIPS

- In the setup of the right-side row, stitch markers of one color are placed before the slipped stitches; all other stitches are knit.

- When working the first wrong-side row, you may choose to place stitch markers before each change in stitch type. While this results in a comically large number of stitch markers, it means that every time a marker is reached, the stitch changes from knit to purl or from purl to knit, and that may relieve you from counting stitches.

- Always change colors at the beginning of a right-side row. To minimize the number of ends that need to be darned in, carry up either MC or CC1, and cut and attach a new supply of CC2 for each repeat. When changing colors, always pick up the new color from underneath the previous color.

- If you're not confident using Kitchener stitch, you can use a standard cast-on for the I-cord edge, and sew the two ends of the I-cord together.

- If a custom-size blanket is desired, each additional repeat adds 4 inches/10cm in width, and, to preserve symmetry, a repeat is added on each side of the center 21 stitches, resulting in an additional 8 inches/20.5cm in width.

- Each additional plaid repeat of the stripe pattern adds 9 inches/23cm in height.

PROVISIONAL CAST-ON

Using the crochet hook and waste yarn, and the crochet provisional cast-on method, CO 149 (225) sts.

SETUP

Row 1 (RS): K16, *pm A, sl 1, (k17, pm A, sl 1) 1 (3) time(s), k10, pm A, sl 1, k17, pm A, sl 1*, k21, repeat from * to *, k16. 8 (12) markers A placed.

Row 2 (WS): Placing a marker B, if desired, so that there is a marker where each comma falls in the instructions: P5, k1, p5, k5, *(p1, k1, p5, k5, p5, k1, p1)* 1 (3) time(s), k10, repeat * to * once, k5, p5, k1, p5, k5, repeat * to * once, k10, repeat * to * 1 (3) time(s), k5, p5, k1, p5.

BOTTOM EDGE

Pattern row 1 (RS): (K to marker A, sl 1 purlwise wyib) 8 (12) times, k to the end.

Pattern row 2 (WS): P5, k1, p5, k5, *(p1, k1, p5, k5, p5, k1, p1)* 1 (3) time(s), k10, repeat * to * once, k5, p5, k1, p5, k5, repeat * to * once, k10, repeat * to * 1 (3) time(s), k5, p5, k1, p5.

Or if you're using marker Bs: (P to marker, k to marker) to the last 5 sts, p to the end.

Work Pattern Rows 1 and 2 three times total in MC. Join CC and work Pattern Rows 1 and 2 once. 5 garter ridges from CO.

BODY

*With MC, work 10 pattern rows—5 repeats of Pattern Rows 1 and 2.

With CC2, work 2 pattern rows.

With CC1, work 10 pattern rows.

With MC, work 2 pattern rows.

With CC1, work 10 pattern rows.

With CC2, work 2 pattern rows.

With MC, work 10 pattern rows.*

With CC1, work 8 pattern rows.

With CC2, work 2 pattern rows.

With CC1, work 8 pattern rows.

Repeat this sequence 2 (4) more times, and then work from * to * once.

TOP EDGE

Starting with the 3 marked sts, work the I-cord bind-off as follows:

*K2, k2tog tbl, sl the resulting 3 sts from the right-hand needle back to the left-hand needle; rep from *, removing markers as you encounter them until all live sts have been worked.

WORK CORNER

(K3, sl 3 sts back onto the left-hand needle) twice.

FIRST LONG SIDE

Using a second supply of MC yarn, leaving a tail to darn in later, and working from the corner where the 3 live sts are held, pick up 3 sts for every 4 rows along the side, and break the new supply of yarn, leaving an ending tail to darn in later. Returning to the corner and using the original working yarn, work the I-cord bind-off as above until all live sts on the side have been worked.

Work a second corner as above.

BOTTOM EDGE

Unpick the crochet chain, place all live sts on the needle, and pick up 1 additional st at the edge. Continuing with the original working yarn, work the I-cord bind-off as above.

Work a third corner as above.

SECOND LONG SIDE

Work as for the first long side with a new supply of yarn.

LAST CORNER

K3, sl 3 sts back onto the left-hand needle.
3 sts remain.

JOIN THE I-CORD STITCHES

Place the 3 sts on the locking st marker onto the empty right-hand needle. Taking care to align both sets of sts, graft the 2 sets of 3 sts together, using Kitchener stitch.

FINISHING

Wash the blanket using tepid water and a wool wash, and lay it flat to dry. Pinning may be helpful to hold the edges flat as the blanket dries, but do not stretch the fabric. Weave in the ends.

HORROCKS'S
Scarf and Blanket

Designed by Holli Yeoh

In episode 9 of season 1, we meet Horrocks, a redcoat deserter who holds the key to clearing Jamie's name of murder but who tries to blackmail him instead. While Horrocks was a nasty piece of work, his scarf was delightful. It served as the inspiration for this blanket and scarf pattern. Simple garter stitch, with some judiciously placed increases and decreases to bend the ridges, turns a plain stitch pattern into something striking.

SKILLS REQUIRED

Picking up stitches

MATERIALS

Berroco Vintage Chunky (52% acrylic, 40% wool, 8% nylon; 136yds/125m per 3.5oz/100g skein); 4 (8, 12, 17) skeins

Sample uses color 6106/Smoke.

Substitution Notes: Look for an airy, bouncy wool blend with easy care instructions.

NEEDLES

US #10/6mm needles for working flat

Or size needed to obtain gauge

NOTIONS

Stitch markers

Yarn needle

GAUGE

14 sts/22 rows = 4 inches/10cm square in stockinette stitch

14 sts/28 rows = 4 inches/10cm square in garter stitch

SIZES

Scarf (Baby Blanket, Lap Blanket, Throw)

FINISHED MEASUREMENTS

Width: 10.5 (32.5, 40, 48) inches/26.5 (82.5, 101.5, 122) cm

Length: 60 (40, 48, 60) inches/152.5 (101.5, 122, 152.5) cm

PATTERN NOTES

This scarf/blanket is worked from the center bottom up. There's a central strip worked in purl garter stitch. The sections to each side of the central strip are worked in garter stitch and on the bias with increases at both ends. Just before the piece reaches its final width, extra stitches are cast on each end for a self-edging. At this time, the center is much longer than the outer edges. Continue working with no additional shaping until the piece reaches its final length. The left upper corner is worked, decreasing stitches toward the outer corner, then the right upper corner is completed in the same manner. Finish by weaving in the ends.

MODIFICATIONS

To make a scarf using this pattern, change the width by determining how many stitches you want for the edge stitches (A). Multiply A by 2 (for both edges) and divide by your stitch gauge to determine their combined width (B). Subtract B from your desired finished width (C). Work Section 1 until it measures C. Proceed to Section 2. To change the length, simply work Section 2 until it measures your desired length.

INSTRUCTIONS

SECTION 1

Using the long-tail cast-on method, cast on 6 (8, 10, 12) sts.

Setup row (WS): K1, pm, p4 (6, 8, 10), pm, k1.

Inc row 1 (RS): K1, p to the marker, kfb. 7 (9, 11, 13) sts.

Inc row 2: K2, p to the marker, kfb. 8 (10, 12, 14) sts.

Inc row 3: K to the marker, M1L, sm, p to the marker, sm, M1R, k to the last st, kfb. 3 sts increased.

Inc row 4: K to the marker, p to the marker, k to the last st, kfb. 1 st increased.

Repeat the last 2 rows 15 (67, 83, 101) times more. 40 (146, 180, 218) sts.

SECTION 2

Row 1 (RS): K to the marker, M1L, sm, p to the marker, sm, M1R, k to the last st, kfb, cast on 3 (4, 5, 5) sts. 46 (153, 188, 226) sts.

Row 2 (WS): P3 (4, 5, 5), k to the marker, p to the marker, k to the last st, kfb, cast on 3 (4, 5, 5) sts. 50 (158, 194, 232) sts.

Row 3: P2 (3, 4, 4), p2tog, k to the marker, M1L, sm, p to the marker, sm, M1R, knit to the last 4 (5, 6, 6) sts, p2tog, p2 (3, 4, 4).

Row 4: P3 (4, 5, 5), k to the marker, p to the marker, knit to the last 3 (4, 5, 5) sts, purl to the end.

Repeat the last 2 rows until the piece measures 60 (40, 48, 60) inches/152.5 (101.5, 122, 152.5) cm, ending with a RS row.

SECTION 3

Setup row (WS): P3 (4, 5, 5), knit to 2 sts before the marker, k2tog; remove the marker, turn and continue on this set of sts only. 22 (75, 92, 110) sts.

Dec row 1 (RS): K to the last 4 (5, 6, 6) sts, p2tog, p2 (3, 4, 4). 1 st decreased.

Dec row 2: P3 (4, 5, 5), k to the last 2 sts, k2tog. 1 st decreased.

Repeat the last 2 rows until 4 (5, 6, 6) sts remain, ending with a WS row.

Next row: Sl 1, p1, psso, bind off remaining sts purlwise.

SECTION 4

With WS facing, rejoin the yarn and pick up and knit 1 st immediately to the right of the sts on the needle, p1, pass the first st over the second st, bind off 3 (5, 7, 9) more sts purlwise, remove marker, k1, pass the second to the last st worked over the last st, knit to the last 3 (4, 5, 5) sts, purl to the end. 21 (74, 91, 109) sts.

Dec row 1 (RS): P2 (3, 4, 4), p2tog, knit to the last 2 sts, k2tog. 2 sts decreased.

Row 2 (WS): Knit to the last 3 (4, 5, 5) sts, purl to the end.

Repeat the last 2 rows until 5 (6, 7, 7) sts remain, ending with a WS row.

Next row (RS): P2 (3, 4, 4), p2tog, k1. 4 (5, 6, 6) sts.

Next row (WS): Sl 1, p1, psso, bind off the remaining sts purlwise.

FINISHING

Wash and lay flat to dry. Weave in the ends.

Glossary and Techniques

Glossary AND Abbreviations

beg — begin(ning)

BO — bind off

BOR — beginning of round

CC — contrasting color

CDD — (centered double decrease): slip 2 sts together as if to knit, knit 1, pass slipped sts over (2 sts decreased)

CO — cast on

dec — decrease(d)(ing)

foll — follow(s)(ing)

inc — increase(d)(ing)

k — knit

k2tog — knit the next 2 sts together (1 st decreased)

k3tog — knit 3 together (2 sts decreased)

kfb — knit into the front and back of the stitch (1 st increased)

kfbf — knit into the front loop, the back loop, and then the front loop, of 1 stitch (2 sts increased)

LLI — (left lifted increase): with the left-hand needle, lift the left leg of the stitch below the stitch just worked, and knit it (1 st increased)

m — marker

M1, M1L — insert the left-hand needle, from front to back, under the strand of yarn that runs between the next stitch on the left-hand needle and the last stitch on the right-hand needle; knit this stitch through the back loop (1 st increased)

M1p — insert the left-hand needle, from front to back, under the strand of yarn that runs between the next stitch on the left-hand needle and the last stitch on right-hand needle; purl this stitch through the back loop (1 st increased)

M1R — insert the left-hand needle, from back to front, under the strand of yarn that runs between the next stitch on the left-hand needle and the last stitch on the right-hand needle; knit this stitch through the front loop (1 st increased)

MC — main color

p — purl

p2sso — pass 2 slipped stitches over the stitch just worked (2 sts decreased)

p2tog — purl 2 stitches together (1 st decreased)

patt(s) — pattern(s)

pfb — purl into the front and back of the stitch (1 st increased)

pm — place marker

rem — remain(ing)

rep — repeat(ing)

RLI — (right lifted increase): with the right-hand needle, lift the right leg of the stitch below the next stitch, and knit into it (1 st increased)

rm — remove marker

RS — right side

sl — slip stitch; stitches should be slipped purlwise unless otherwise noted

sm — slip marker

ssk — slip the next 2 stitches, one-by-one, knitwise; insert the tip of the left-hand needle, from left to right, into the fronts of those 2 stitches and knit them together (1 st decreased)

sssk slip the next 3 stitches, one by one, knitwise; insert the tip of the left-hand needle, from left to right, into the fronts of those 3 stitches and knit them together. (2 sts decreased)

St st stockinette stitch

st(s) stitch(es)

tbl through the back of a loop or loops

w&t (wrap & turn): slip the next stitch onto the right-hand needle, take the yarn to the opposite side of the work between the needles, slip the same stitch back onto the left-hand needle. Turn the work so you're ready to begin working in the opposite direction.

WS wrong side

wyib with yarn in back

wyif with yarn in front

yo yarnover; bring the yarn to the front between the tips of the needles and let it drape over the needle for the next stitch (1 st increased)

Techniques AND References

BACKWARDS LOOP CAST-ON

Make a twisted (e-wrap) loop with the working yarn and place on the needle.

CABLE CAST-ON

*Insert needle between the first 2 sts on the left-hand needle, pull the yarn through to form a st, then place the new st on the left-hand needle; rep from * until the desired number of sts have been cast on.

GERMAN SHORT ROWS

Create a double stitch (abbreviated as DS) at the turn point: once the last stitch of the previous row is worked, turn the work. Bring the working yarn to the front and slip that just-worked stitch purlwise onto the right-hand needle. Tug on the working yarn, bringing it up and over the needle, around the back, so that the just-worked stitch is pulled up tight, and two strands are sitting on the needle. If you're going to knit the next stitch, leave the yarn at the back, keeping the tension, and work back in pattern. If you're going to purl the next stitch, bring it around the needle to the front, as if for a yarnover, maintaining the tension.

This creates what look like doubled stitches, stitches with two legs up on the needle. When you encounter one of these on a subsequent row, just work into it as normal, catching the two strands.

Tin Can Knits Tutorial: https://blog.tincanknits .com/2015/05/14/german-short-rows/

I-CORD BIND-OFF

Using your preferred method, CO 3 sts at the start of the row.

Row 1 (RS): K2, ssk, turn. Return these 2 sts back onto the left-hand needle and repeat the row, pulling the yarn tight across the back to make an I-cord.

knitpurlhunter.com/blog/i-cord-bind-off/

KITCHENER STITCH/GRAFTING

knitty.com/ISSUEss18/FEATss18WK/FEATss-18WK.php

Cut the yarn, leaving a tail of about four times the width of the seam to be joined. Hold the needles parallel, with the work hanging down—as if for a three-needle bind-off, with the WS together, and the RS of the front piece facing you.

With the yarn tail threaded onto a yarn needle, work as follows:

THE SETUP
Front needle: Thread the needle through the first stitch purlwise, and pull the yarn through.

Back needle: Thread the needle through the first stitch knitwise, and pull the yarn through.

THE REPEAT
Front needle: Thread the needle through the first stitch knitwise, slip the stitch off, pull the yarn through. Thread the needle through the next stitch purlwise, leave the stitch on the needle, pull the yarn through.

Back needle: Thread the needle through the first stitch purlwise, slip the stitch off, pull the yarn through. Thread the needle through the next stitch knitwise, leave the stitch on the needle, pull the yarn through.

THE LAST STEP

Front needle: Thread the needle through the last stitch knitwise, slip the stitch off, pull the yarn through.

Back needle: Thread the needle through the last stitch purlwise, slip the stitch off, pull the yarn through.

~~~~~~~~~~~~~~~~~~~~~~~~~~~

LONG-TAIL CAST-ON

http://knitty.com/ISSUEw18/FEATw18WK/FEATw18WK.php

~~~~~~~~~~~~~~~~~~~~~~~~~~~

MODIFIED ICELANDIC BIND-OFF

strandsoflife.com/modified-icelandic-bind-off

~~~~~~~~~~~~~~~~~~~~~~~~~~~

PROVISIONAL CAST-ON

With waste yarn, make a slip knot and place it on a crochet hook. Bring the knitting needle to the left of your crochet hook, with the yarn from the skein underneath the needle. Take the crochet hook over the needle and hook the yarn, bringing it back over the needle and through the loop onto the crochet hook. Move the yarn from the skein back underneath the needle and repeat this process until the desired number of stitches have been cast on.

An excellent photo tutorial by Tin Can Knits can be found at: blog.tincanknits.com/2015/07/16/provisional-cast-on-needle-and-hook-method/

~~~~~~~~~~~~~~~~~~~~~~~~~~~

THREE-NEEDLE BIND-OFF

Holding the two left-hand needles parallel to each other, insert the right-hand needle into the first stitch on the front needle as if to knit, then insert it through the first stitch on the back needle as if to knit. Knit the stitch as normal, pulling the yarn through both stitches and pulling the stitches off the left-hand needles. *Knit the next stitch from each left-hand needle the same way, pass the first stitch on the right-hand needle back over the second stitch; repeat from * as for a regular bind-off.

~~~~~~~~~~~~~~~~~~~~~~~~~~~

TWISTED GERMAN CAST-ON

youtube.com/watch?v=BfFadEumBak

~~~~~~~~~~~~~~~~~~~~~~~~~~~

YARNOVER BIND-OFF METHOD

masondixonknitting.com/techniques-in-depth-bind-off-loosely/

ABOUT
the Designers

✕✕✕✕✕✕

Anne Blayney

ravelry.com/designers/anne-blayney

Anne is a conference planner at a Canadian think tank by day, and an occasional knitting designer in her spare time. She is at least 85 percent milky tea by volume, so the chance to design a cozy to keep her tea warm in all seasons was especially welcome.

Maya Bosworth

ravelry.com/designers/maya-bosworth

Maya's mother taught her to knit when she was a child, but it took until she was in her late thirties before she fell in love with knitting. After many years without knitting a thing, she started dabbling in the craft again. Soon after, a friend told her about Etsy and that's when she decided to try her hand at designing hats to sell. She realized that she could also sell the patterns and has since had designs commissioned by the yarn company Scheepjes and *Knit Now* magazine. Knitting gives Maya a lot of satisfaction; she also finds it endlessly fascinating. She likes how it's both ancient and modern—it has history and tradition yet it's still so new and fresh.

Eimear Earley

ravelry.com/designers/playing-with-fiber

Eimear originally learned to knit as a schoolchild, and dabbled with leftover yarn, without any concept of gauge or ease during her teenage years. Formerly a craft design student who played

with molten glass, she now gets her creative kicks from knitting and spinning wool—much more practical pursuits. Eimear loves to reinterpret old Irish things into modern knitwear, from ancient gold artifacts to less ancient cable knitting. Her favorite fiber to work with is wool. She lives in Ireland, where she spends most of her time taking care of two small humans, and also likes to drink an awful lot of tea, preferably warm.

Cheryl Eaton

behindtheivy.co.uk

Cheryl loves inspiring creative moments. She lives and knits along the northeast coast of England, and enjoys exploring the woodlands and beaches that surround her home.

After first learning to knit when she was little, Cheryl picked up the needles again some fifteen years later and an obsession was born. She is particularly fond of knitting socks. They are the perfect practical knit—hard-wearing, useful, beautiful, and cozy, hand-knit socks are the ultimate portable project and are a great canvas for experimenting with new techniques and ideas.

Anni Howard

annihoward.com

Anni is an independent knit and textile designer working from her studio in Colchester in the UK, close to the Essex estuaries and coastal salt marshes. The faded colors and rich textures of her local landscape have found their way into

Anni's Ebb and Flow collection of designs, which are available from Ravelry and Love Crafts. After obtaining a degree in textiles, Anni worked at a yarn spinning company before collaborating with yarn and fiber companies and magazines. She is inspired by repeating patterns, textures, colors, unusual knitting techniques, and interesting garment constructions.

MARY HULL

kinoknits.com

Mary picked up the first *Outlander* book while visiting her aunt at age sixteen; since she couldn't take the book with her, she read the whole thing in twenty-four hours—and several times since then. Mary is the designer and podcaster behind Kino Knits and aims to guide knitters and listeners along interesting paths to intriguing destinations. She hasn't managed to master time travel yet.

NICKY JENSEN

handknitsandhygge.com

Nicky has been knitting and crocheting for over twenty-five years. Recently, she discovered a passion for knitwear design after enrolling in a course to keep her occupied during her maternity leave (as if the baby wouldn't be enough). She lives in Toronto, Canada, with her husband, dog, and baby girl, where, when she's not designing, she works as a medical radiation technologist.

MIEKA JOHN

saltandstoneknits.com

Mieka, of Salt & Stone Knits, is a knitwear designer whose passion is diving into new techniques and using them to develop designs inspired by her travels around the world. Originally from New York City, she now lives in beautiful Amsterdam, spending her days discovering her creativity and biking to the next appointment with a basket full of WIPs. When she

moved to the Netherlands, her hands clung to the crafts she had learned as a child. With each stitch she found comfort, found her community, and slowly made a new country feel like home.

BARRY KLEIN

ravelry.com/designers/barry-klein

One of the founders of Trendsetter Yarns, Barry is also a skilled knitting designer and teacher.

SARAH LEHTO

ravelry.com/designers/sarah-lehto

Sarah is a lover of all things fibery. Her grandma taught her to knit in 2004 and she's been obsessed with knitting ever since, adding in spinning, weaving, dyeing, and crochet to her repertoire through the years. She lives with her husband and two daughters in northern Minnesota and dreams of owning a fiber farm.

JANELLE MARTIN

eclecticcloset.ca

Janelle is part of the management team for Learning for Humanity, a social enterprise that provides eLearning-managed systems for the developing world. Her creative outlet is teaching knitting classes and designing knitwear inspired by the geometry and patterns of the natural world. She fell deeply in love with Japanese stitch patterns in the mid-2000s and still hasn't recovered.

JESSIE McKITRICK

grammargrouse.blogspot.com

Jessie lives in Edmonton, Alberta, Canada, with her husband, daughters, three gerbils, and lots of wool. If she's not knitting, she's spinning yarn, reading, or practicing karate.

Jessie writes patterns for hand-knitters who can't resist the lure of texture, cables, and color in their

next sweater, hat, or mitten project. Her patterns can be found through Interweave Knits, *Knit Now* magazine, Ancient Arts Yarns, Knit Picks, and her Ravelry shop.

CLAIRE NEICHO

ravelry.com/designers/claire-neicho
Originally from England, Claire moved to the island of Whalsay, one of the Shetland Islands, in 2010. Inspired by the tremendous skills of the local knitters, Claire soon learned to knit Fair Isle in the traditional way, using long DPNs and a knitting belt. Although Claire had previously

been a knitter, it was learning to knit Fair Isle that reinforced a love for the craft, and in 2013 Claire began designing and writing knitting patterns for both magazines and self-publishing, specializing in Fair Isle and stranded colorwork patterns. Claire's work reflects both the rich knitting heritage of Shetland and the Shetland landscape.

LYNNE SOSNOWSKI

ravelry.com/designers/lynne-sosnowski
After a career of producing large-scale municipal festivals and events, Lynne now splits her time between designing knitwear, teaching knitting

classes that specialize in "knit literacy," and producing stand-up comedy festivals and live shows. She's funny for a regular person.

KATHLEEN SPERLING

wipinsanity.com

Kathleen learned to knit when she was seven or eight years old, and did it occasionally while growing up. She didn't become seriously obsessed with knitting until adulthood, when she started making baby knits for friends who were expecting—these were the gateway projects to discovering all the wonderful techniques that knitting has to offer! Then she found that she loved designing. Knitting inspires her with ideas for a wide variety of patterns and people. She particularly loves colorwork, and adapting inspiration pieces into knitting, and so, of course, very much enjoyed designing for this collection!

ALLISON THISTLEWOOD

champagneandqiviut.com

Allison is a champion of indie makers and creative small businesses in the yarn and fiber community. Based in the UK, she's worn a lot of different hats in the yarn industry since relocating from Canada seven years ago. From sales rep for luxury yarn and notions brands to communications and marketing consultant for designers and yarn shops, content development, PR, and event planning, Allison shares her adventures in the yarn community through her blog Champagne & Qiviut. Allison currently works for an arts not-for-profit outside London as the events coordinator for craft.

KARIE WESTERMANN

kariebookish.net

Karie is a Danish-Scottish knitwear designer, writer, and teacher. She lives in beautiful Glasgow, Scotland, with her husband (who happens to be a member of Clan Fraser himself). Karie's work combines her Scandinavian love of storytelling with the Scottish love of colorplay and knitting traditions. In her book, *This Thing of Paper: Eleven Knitting Patterns Inspired by Books*, she took medieval manuscripts and libraries as her inspiration. In her spare time, Karie loves reading, art, dressmaking, and meeting friendly dogs.

ANTHEA WILLIS

ravelry.com/designers/anthea-willis

Anthea is a knit designer who just loves to play with textures and stitch patterns to create practical, classic (and sometimes a little whimsical) pieces to be worn and loved for years to come. Inspiration comes from her study of history and archaeology, a love of the wild, the beautiful Forest of Dean she calls home, and the wonderful wooly yarn stash that, despite her best efforts to keep it under control, seems to be gradually taking over the tiny house she shares with her partner, their son, and various feline companions . . .

HOLLI YEOH

holliyeoh.com

Holli's passion for knitting has spanned a lifetime, from learning to knit as a child to her fine arts degree, majoring in textiles and jewelry, and an eighteen-year designing career. A Holli Yeoh pattern is sure to offer something to learn, as well as a casually elegant aesthetic. Interesting techniques and clear instructions ensure a rewarding knit with beautiful results, as featured in leading publications and her book *Tempest*. See more of Holli's work at holliyeoh.com.

Acknowledgments

This book couldn't have happened without the support of . . .
Angelin Borsics, Gabrielle Van Tassel, Patricia Shaw, Heather
Williamson, Francesca Truman, Marysarah Quinn, and Diana Drew at
Clarkson Potter. Barry Klein and Anita Bivens at Trendsetter Yarns
who provided yarn and championed the book on a grassroots level. At
Sony Pictures, Virginia King.

Our photographer, Gale Zucker; her assistant, Yliana Tibitoski;
and our gorgeous models Ariana McLean, Jack Hobbs, and Laura
Troitskite. The owners Dawn and Ken of the Windy Cottage in
Granby, Connecticut, where the project photographs were taken.

Our other yarn providers: Berroco Yarns and Sweet Georgia Yarns.
Our designers: Anne Blayney, Maya Bosworth, Eimear Earley, Cheryl
Eaton, Anni Howard, Mary Hull, Nicky Jensen, Mieka John, Barry
Klein, Sarah Lehto, Janelle Martin, Jessie McKitrick, Claire Neicho,
Lynne Sosnowski, Kathleen Sperling, Allison Thistlewood, Karie
Westermann, Anthea Willis, and Holli Yeoh.

On a personal note, I'd like to thank Patricia Shaw and my
husband, Norman Wilner.

Index